Ber

Mer

Slightly belated —

Love —

BLUE TRUTH

BLUE TRUTH

Walking the Thin Blue Line
—One Cop's Story
of Life In the Streets

Cherokee Paul McDonald

DONALD I. FINE, INC.
New York

Library of Congress Cataloging-in-Publication Data

McDonald, Cherokee Paul.
Blue truth / Cherokee Paul McDonald.
p. cm.
ISBN 1–55611–246–7
1. McDonald, Cherokee Paul.   2. Police–Florida–Fort Lauderdale–
Biography.   I. Title.
HV7911.M356A3   1991
363.2'092—dc20
[B]   90-56070
                                                                    CIP

Manufactured in the United States of America

10   9   8   7   6   5   4   3   2   1

This book is dedicated to
John C. Alexander
and
Kenneth Petersen,
who died on duty, 3 August, 1981

Note

This is a work of nonfiction. All persons and events described herein are real and are portrayed as accurately as memory allows. Because perspective and perception differ from eye to eye, and to protect the right to privacy of the police officers and victims... and criminals... involved, all names of persons described in this work are pseudonyms.

CPMc

Apologize?

Me . . . *apologize?*

Let me give you a little hint:

Never.

Even when I did the wrong thing,

I

did

it

for

the

right

reason.

Foreword

A MOMENT ago the cop stood in a room surrounded by death. The bodies were those of an entire family, man, woman, and children. It was too soon to tell if it was the work of some serial killer, or just a murder-suicide. Now he leans into your car window to speak with you about the traffic ticket he is writing out. You notice he is polite but determined, and has a potbelly straining the front of his otherwise neat uniform.

A moment ago the cop leaned over a man having a heart attack in a grocery store parking lot. The sun beat down on the cop's back as her mouth opened over the victim's, forcing in hot breaths of frightened air. When the victim gagged, the mess bubbled out onto the cop's face and collar, but still the breaths were given. The cop cleaned herself up after the ambulance took the victim away, and now she stands in the clutter of your ransacked bedroom. You have called the police to report a burglary, and as the cop takes notes for her paperwork she seems almost cold, and you feel the color of her nails is inappropriate for someone in an official capacity.

In a few moments both cops will walk into the darkened gloom of a filthy crackhouse in search of a diseased and coked-out rapist. They will have their service weapons drawn, their lips will be dry, and they will know fear.

For most cops there are times when they will have to do something because no one else will, and they work in the knowledge that every day on the job has the potential for being the last.

I left the Fort Lauderdale Police Department after ten years, and carried with me an uncompromising desire to communicate things I had seen and learned. The human being in me had felt almost invisible and mute as a cop, my frustration at being unable to speak to you was total, and after laying down the gun and badge I embraced the written word to record those times that had had such great impact on me. Ten years have passed since then, and during that time I have carried these stories in my mind and heart, bringing them out of their protective hiding places to fit them into readable (thus audible and visible) order. To live as I wrote I took odd jobs on boats, toiled as a night watchman, did personal security and salvage work, and spent my energies pounding on an old standard typewriter, to save the memories of police work that burned the most.

I was raised and schooled in Fort Lauderdale, Florida. I joined the FLPD after returning home from serving with the army in Vietnam. I was a Fort Lauderdale cop from 1970 to 1980, and during those ten years I was assigned, in addition to various road patrol shifts, to the Harbor Patrol, Traffic Division (Motorman), Communications, Administration (Crime Analysis), experimental antismuggling reaction teams (marine), and as undercover narcotics officer in a countywide task force. I ended my career as a sergeant, assigned to Patrol Division. I left in good standing, and still maintain my status as a Certified Police Officer in the State of Florida.

As a working police officer I received over twenty public, city, departmental, and state commendations, including Officer of the Month and nominee for Officer of the Year. I also received several written and permanent reprimands and disciplinary transfers, and twice I was suspended without pay as punishment for what was determined to be improper actions on my part. My personnel file evaluations describe me as "professional," "aggressive," and "a credit to the department." I was respected as a supervisor, and was active in the Fraternal Order of Police, assigned to committees concerned with the welfare of injured officers. Too late I realized I had failed to protectively separate the inner me from the outer professional police officer.

Things I saw and did scarred me, weakened my idealism, and left me vulnerable. It was time to walk away from it, but how do you walk away from yourself?

When people observed me in my uniform, on the street, they saw a shirt and badge, a faceless and heartless representative of authority. But like all cops, I was in there, flesh and blood and heart. They are in there, behind what is often mistakingly called a "shield." They hear you and see you, and they know and feel the feelings you experience because *they* feel them too.

The stories in this book are true. I wrote them to share with you, who are not police officers, so you could see some small glimpses of their truth, and with you who *are* police officers, so you could know that many things that have affected you have affected others.

The cop you see sitting in a doughnut shop, racing code-three to a drowning victim, reading a newspaper in a squad car, or facing off against a violent armed robber is a *person*.

Some days cops are heroes, occasionally they are not, but always they are human.

CPMc
Fort Lauderdale, 1990

One

IT WAS a hard metal trinity . . . the badge, the gun, and the handcuffs. Each was cold and heavy with inherent power and responsibility, each was forged with precise purpose.

The handcuffs were twin loops of unyielding steel brought together by locking ratchet teeth which encircled the wrists of those whose immediate freedom I arrested. The gun was a Smith &Wesson Model Ten .38 Calibre revolver, blue steel with wooden grips. It was a beautifully machined thing, with a firm trigger squeeze, smoothly spinning cylinder, and comfortable weight. It came to the palm of my hand like it had been waiting all of our lives, and it was with a sense of controlled urgency and power that the six semi-jacketed 158–grain bullets slid into the cylinder, there to wait for their turn in the breech of the barrel for the impact of the firing pin. The gun was cold blue steel which leapt to my hand and warmed to its task when bidden. The badge could be all things to one who was young, naive, idealistic, and thirsty for the truth. It too had weight, not just symbolically, but in the palm of my hand, and on my shirt. It hung there shiny and proud, sharp-edged and hard. Mine was silver, and it glowed with a richness and depth that I understood came from the fact that infused in it was the power, the authority, the law, the right, the hope, the faith, the good, and the invulnerability it represented.

I wore that hard metal trinity as part of my Fort Lauderdale police uniform the day I stood at proud attention and graduated with the thirty-third police academy class in Broward County.

The virginal handcuffs lay coiled in their leather pouch, still unaware of the taste of angry sweat or the pull of resisting tendons. The gun rode in its holster, waiting, confident, a passive judge in condescending repose. And on my chest, stroked by the rhythmic beating of my heart, lay the badge. It was pinned to the fabric of my uniform shirt, and it summed up with a singular clarity everything I had worked for, stood for, and represented. It was my identity, my reason, my passport to the truth.

And what of the flesh and blood that was me?

I was a young soldier come home, curiously aged by a war I did not yet know I had lost. Battle had triggered something in me, fueled by the sure knowledge that I had fought for the right, the good. I liked soldiering against evil, I liked taking up arms and pitting myself against an enemy who would do bad things to good people. I came home to the only war in town, the only battle I could soldier in, the field of struggle where the good side needed me, where an identifiable enemy could be met in physical combat and defeated. I came home to the street.

I had looked for truth in the war I had come from, and many times felt I had found it, or some of it . . . but there was still an undefined doubt in the core of me. Now, I knew, I would find the truth. I was certified by the state as a police officer. I was graduating from the academy and within days I would be working the streets as a member of my own hometown police department. I had listened in fascination and with acceptance to the lessons presented during the academy term. I had no doubt that I had been more than adequately prepared for what awaited me. I respected those learned and experienced older cops who had been there and then came to teach me. They had seen the battlefield, and they described it for me as I sat rigid in my seat absorbing the impact of their words.

I had heard the truth in their words. I carried the truth on my hip, and wore it on my chest. I wrapped myself in that truth, girded my loins and my heart with that hard metal trinity, and went forward to do battle on the hot streets of home.

Two

I HAD taken a wife while I was in the police academy, and we had set up our home in a trailer park. We were consumed with the proximity and unlimited accessibility of each other's bodies, and during the brief moments of rest we would gaze out at the unknown world and future through a mist of complacency and ignorance. When it was time for me to go in for my first active duty, on day shift, my wife helped me zip and pin and buckle my gear on, packed me a brown-bag lunch as if I were on my way to a construction job, and sent me off smiling. At that point "the street" might as well have been the surface of Mars.

So I was a brand new patrolman on day shift, riding the central section of the city with an older officer. The central section had the downtown area, with all the shops and department stores, and across the tracks it had the "black section." I had come from a lower middle-class home where both parents worked hard all their lives and the old values were taught and adhered to. My father had taught me that all men should be treated as equals until one learned about each individual man— then they could be judged. I never used the word "nigger."

The older officer and I were riding along, shooting the breeze, when suddenly a couple of blocks away we saw dust in the air and people running and then over the radio we heard one of the traffic units yelling about a black male running west from the scene of an accident. My partner accelerated and turned onto the next street, heading west. As we approached Seventh Avenue he yelled at me, "That nigger probably didn't have his goddamned driver's license, or maybe he stole the fuckin' car. Let's get him!" I sat there trying to hang onto the door, and as we shot out onto Seventh Avenue sure enough there was this young black guy about my age and size running as hard as he could across the street and through a vacant lot between a couple of small businesses. My partner drove up to the curb, slammed on the brakes, and yelled, "You go after him on foot, kid. I'll tell the other units you're in pursuit, and follow along in the car!"

Totally consumed with the excitement of it all, I bailed out and went running after the black guy as hard as I could. I was just crossing the field as I saw him run left down one alley and then head west again in another alley. I followed and watched as he headed across the next street and into the open bay doors of one of the warehouse businesses there. As he vanished into the shadows I went hurdling across the street, right in front of some guy in a station wagon who slammed on his brakes, leaned out the window, and screamed at me.

As I ran into the front bay of the business I could not see the black guy, but two men who were standing by some crates yelled at me and pointed to the open rear bay door, which led into another alley. I ran by them and out into the alley in time to see the black guy climb up on a dumpster and jump across an old wooden fence into the rear of another business. As he jumped into the air I saw him turn and look at me with his mouth open and his eyes wide. For the first time I noticed he was wearing black pants, a black shirt, and a black jacket. While I was thinking how odd it was to wear a jacket in that heat I saw he was carrying something in his hand, but didn't give it any thought. As he hit the ground and fell I yelled at him, "Halt, *police*! Stop right there!"

As I jumped up on the dumpster I saw him get to his knees, look at me, stand up, and lurch off again, slower this time, but still running hard toward the west. I jumped the fence, hit, rolled, and ran after him, thinking he sure was desperate over a simple traffic violation. I rounded the corner of the business in time to see him run across another street, heading for a group of green apartments on Ninth Avenue. As I ran behind him I watched as he stripped off his jacket and then his shirt as he ran. I yelled, "Halt, *police!*" again, and as he turned to look at me he stumbled and almost fell, but recovered. From where I was I could see that he was sweating heavily, and his face was ashen.

I was still running strong and feeling good, not tired, but hampered by all of my gear. The leather gunbelt restricted my stride, and the gun in its holster flopped up and down against my leg as I ran. I felt as if my uniform were made of burlap bags, it sort of wrapped around me and stuck there in the heat. I watched the black guy from about fifty yards back as he stuck something into a hedge at the corner of one of the green apartments and then vanished around the edge of the building. I ran up to the corner as hard as I could and was trying to remember if I should stop and look slowly around the corner or just go ahead and barrel on around it and hope for the best. My speed and leather shoes on the grass made the decision for me and I skidded around at full speed and finally confronted the black guy face to face. Sort of.

To the rear of the green apartments ran a ten-foot chain-link fence topped with three strands of barbed wire. The black guy had attempted to climb it using a small Florida holly tree for support. He had made it to the top of the chain-link but then became hopelessly entwined in the barbed wire. Exhausted, he had finally lost his grip, and he was now hanging over the fence head down, legs wrapped in the wire.

I yelled, "*Freeze!*" and stood there looking at him.

He looked around and croaked, "Don't shoot me man, don't shoot me . . ." I walked over to the fence and looked at his face six inches from mine, and said, "Shoot you? I'm not gonna shoot you, man, I just want you to stop running from me, okay?" He didn't say anything so I stepped back and climbed up the holly tree to the top of the fence, where I pulled on the wire around his legs. He began squirming around so I said, "Now listen, guy. When I get you out of here I want you to sit down there by that fence and wait until I get to that side. Don't be running off again or I'll just have to keep chasing you, and you know other officers are chasing you too." He still didn't say anything and I looked around and still didn't see any other cops. We had covered a lot of ground fast, and since I had no radio there was no way they could know where I was. I saw that a small group of black people was gathering at the rear of the apartments. They talked and gestured but I couldn't hear what they said. I tried again to free the black guy's legs from the wire but his own weight was working against him so I climbed over the wire myself and jumped down to the other side where he was hanging. As I did so my left hand slid across the barbed wire and I tore a two-inch gash across the palm. This started to bleed a lot of bright red blood that ran down my fingers and up my arm as I moved it around.

Once I was down on the ground I tried to lift the guy up but even with him squirming around it wasn't enough to free him so I turned and saw a large round black woman standing a few feet behind me. She just stood there watching with her heavy arms crossed against her ample chest. She wore a pair of stretch shorts and a sleeveless blouse, and she had those pink rubber curlers in her hair. I looked at her and said, "Excuse me, ma'am. I need some help here. Could you please go inside and call the police and tell them I'm back here with this guy we were chasing? Give them your address and tell them I'm back here, okay?" She didn't say anything, just looked at me and then the guy hanging in the wire. Then she slowly turned and walked away.

I looked at the black guy hanging there and said, "Well, if I can get some more guys here we'll get you down in a minute." He hung there with his eyes closed, sweating and breathing hard. "Why are you running from me anyway, man?" I asked, and he hung there, silent. We stayed like that for what seemed like a long time, neither one saying anything, and him bucking and twisting violently once in a while.

Finally I heard sirens and then racing car engines and tires squealing and brakes skidding and then there were guys yelling and the next thing I knew the entire area of the green apartments was full of police officers, all running as hard as they could toward me.

As the first cops got to me they were yelling, "All right, kid! You *got* him kid! All right!" and as they came up to me they saw the bright red blood covering my hand and arm and they went wild. "He's *hurt!* He's bleedin'!" One of the motorcycle officers grabbed me and pulled me away from the fence and twisted my palm up, saying, "Here, kid, let me look at that." I looked at all the cops still arriving and asked, "What's going on? How'd you guys find me?" The motorman pushed his helmet back on his head and said, "Some woman called in and gave her address, said there was a cop hurt and he needed help, so here we are." I looked around at all the guys heading for the fence and said under my breath, "Holy shit!"

The first cops to get to the fence grabbed the black guy's arms and screamed, "Okay you badass black motherfucker... it's payback time!" and "You gonna die now nigger!" and "You *cut* a cop, nigger? You *crazy* nigger?" and stuff like that. Then they literally ripped him out of the wire and off the fence and began beating him into the grass and dirt. I could hear the black guy screaming, "No, no, noooo!" and his grunts and curses as the fists rained down on him. Suddenly someone hissed, "Cool it, the brass!" and the next time I looked the black guy was laying on his stomach with his hands handcuffed behind him. There was blood all over his face, and his hair was full of dirt. Another cop ran up with a first aid kit and as he got out a compress for my hand a captain looked at it and said, "Looks like you'll need some stitches, kid, but you did a fine job, real fine. The chief will be here in a minute." As he walked away I looked at the other cop and said, "The chief? He's coming here for a traffic violator? I mean... I'm not really hurt that bad..." The other cop looked at me and grinned, saying, "Hell, kid, you're a hero. Shit yeah, that dumbass nigger just pulled an armed robbery of a drug store, fired a couple of shots into the place, and then got into an accident a couple of blocks away. The jerk ran a stop sign and crashed into another car right in front of one of our accident investigators. Then he hauled ass and you chased him and caught him. So you're a hero." I looked at him, then the black guy laying on the ground, and shook my head.

I watched as one of the detectives went through the black guy's pockets and just as the chief and some other brass walked up the detective stood and held up a large roll of money. The chief looked at the black guy, the money, then over at me. He asked, "You okay, kid?" and I puffed myself up and said, "Yessir. Guess I'll just need a couple of stitches, sir." The chief nodded and smiled and looked down at the black guy on the ground again and then at the crowd of people gathering nearby and stopped smiling. He said something to one of the captains and the next thing I knew the black guy was lifted off the ground and whisked out to one of the units on the street. The detective came over to me and asked, "Did you see him drop or throw anything, kid?" I told him about the shirt and jacket, but they had already recovered those, so I told him about the bushes at the corner of the apartments on the other side of the fence. He yelled at one of the cops milling around on the other side and the cop and several others huddled around the bushes at the corner, and shouted when they found what they searched for. The cache was then passed over the fence to the detective, and I noticed that the chief had come over and was standing behind me. The detective said, "Here ya go, kid," and handed me a plastic baggie containing a small metal bottle cap, a silver spoon burnt on one end, and a hypodermic needle. Then he held up a small black revolver. I looked at it wide-eyed as he said, "I bet it's got two expended rounds and four live ones still in the chamber." I didn't say anything but in a flash my mind went over the chase and I saw very clearly at least three places where the black guy could have waited and killed me with his little black gun. And he was a junkie.

Suddenly I was very scared.

The chief said, "Say, son, you look pale. Maybe you should get on over to the emergency room now for those stitches." He clapped me on the shoulder and said, "Fine job, son...just fine."

A few hours later I was feeling better. They had taken great care of me at the ER and everyone was treating me with deference and I was beginning to like being a hero. I went up to the jail to sign the booking slip and when I arrived I saw the black guy sitting on one of the hard gray benches against the wall behind the bars in the holding area. I saw that most of the blood had been washed off him but that his face was swollen and his lips were split in a couple of places. His face was ashen and his eyes were watery. I don't think he recognized me. The old booking sergeant waddled over beside me and said in his gravelly voice, "I hear you did a good job out there, kid. Look at him, already getting the shakes. He'll be screamin' for a fix in a couple of hours. Real badass." I looked at the black guy and saw that he had wrapped his arms around himself and was starting to shivver. I got the paperwork squared away and as I got ready to leave the old sergeant came over to me and said, "Ya know...it's hard to figure with these guys. Damn junkies. This kid didn't hardly have any juvenile record at all, and he just got out of the army a while back according to his papers. I asked him about it and he said he had been in Vietnam. Found his DD214 crumpled up in his wallet. You know that junkie sonofabitch came home from there with a Purple Heart and a Bronze Star with 'V'? Look at him. Who would believe it? Just look at him."

I looked at him. I looked at him and saw me. He was just a black reflection of me, same age, same build, same upbringing, same military experience.

He was just my negative.

I looked at him, a young black robber-junkie. Then I turned and walked out, a young white cop-hero.

Three

"Officer, tell us again how you came to stop the defendant in the first place. I mean, what did he do that made you feel you could detain him and 'check him out,' as you say?"

"Well, sure. I was talking with some of the guys coming off midnight shift and they told me to look for him because they were pretty sure he had done the smash and grab at Davie Boulevard and Twenty-seventh Avenue."

"They were 'pretty sure'?"

"Yeah, you know... they had seen him in the area earlier and they know the way he usually works..."

"Now wait a minute, officer, all this is hearsay. How much of this do *you* know personally?"

"Well, I know who he is and I know he is one of the neighborhood burglars..."

"And just how do you know that? Have you ever seen him burglarize any place?"

"No, I haven't. But hell, everybody knows he's been into this stuff since he was a kid. He even used to be on a list that the juvenile squad put out."

"Do you have that list with you?"

"No."

"Okay, please go on. Tell us why you stopped the defendant."

"Like I said, the midnight guys told me to be on the lookout for him and a little while later I observed him scootin' through an alley. His hair was longer then and he was wearing jeans

10

and a windbreaker. 'He kept lookin' all around, you know . . .
hinky."

"Hinky?"

"Yeah, you know, hinky . . . acting nervous, not right. So I
called to him to stop and he got that look like he was gonna
rabbit but I came up . . ."

"Hold it, officer. How far from him were you when you first
saw him?"

"Across the street."

"And from there you could tell he was, as you say, 'hinky'?
From there you could tell he was going to, as you say, 'rabbit'?"

"Yeah."

"How could you tell these things, officer?"

"You know . . . the way he looked. I could just tell, that's all."

"So you decided to accost him there in the alley. Stop him,
detain him, force him to submit to a search? Is that right?"

"Yeah. that's right."

"And you claim he had a camera under his jacket? And a
baggie of what you claim to be marijuana in his pants pocket?
Right?"

"Well, yeah. I was told to look for him, I saw him. He was
hinky so I patted him down . . . you know, 'for his protection
and mine.' That's when I found the camera, it could have been
a weapon under his jacket. And the baggie of grass made a
pretty good bulge in his pants pocket so I thought I'd better
check it out. The camera was stolen during the smash and
grab . . ."

"Yes, officer. Do you know where the defendant got the camera? Didn't he tell you he found it in the alley?"

"Well, sure, but . . ."

"But nothing, officer. I have no further questions of this witness, Your Honor, and at this time I would like to ask that the
court consider the facts; that in actuality this officer had no
real basis, legal or otherwise, to stop and detain the defendant.
Then he illegally searched him and charged him with the narcotics charge and possession of stolen property. At this time I

ask the court to find that these charges stem from the product of an illegal search, and that they be dropped immediately."

"The court concurs, Mr. Counselor. And before we adjourn I want to take a moment to warn you, officer, that what you do out on the street must conform with the law. You can't just do what you please out there. You must work within those guidelines so clearly set out for you. Don't get carried away so much with trying to do the right thing that you violate a man's rights, as you have in this incident.

"Well, officer, don't you have anything to say?"

Four

OFTEN IN the early days I would come home from the street or the hallways of the courthouse and tell my wife everything that had happened, all of the indignities I and the truth had suffered, all of the bullshit we waded through. To me it was a sharing of matters of importance. I shared them with her because they were becoming the air that I breathed.

She cared for me, tried to comfort me, but had a mind of her own, so she couldn't help but say things like, "But you're like a frontline soldier of the judicial system, right? Your job ends after the arrest . . . then you can walk away and not care what the court does with the case. This young man you arrested might make it with another chance. The insurance companies will pay for the stolen stuff, and who really gives a damn about some kid smoking grass anyway? Listen, don't take it so personally . . . just let it slide."

She would rub my back to relax me. We would make love

and she would rub me more until she fell asleep, and I would lie there staring at the ceiling, going over it, wondering where I had blown it and what I could do next time to make it better. I would look at her in the dark and watch her sleeping. She was beautiful, but my inner heart already whispered to me that our state of comparative conscience could easily be defined by where we both were at that moment . . . my searching eyes were wide open, staring, and I was fitfully awake. Her eyes were closed in naive acceptance, and she was peacefully asleep.

Five

I WAS working a midnight shift in the northeast part of town, riding by myself, still relatively new. As I headed east on Sunrise Boulevard toward the beach I saw a new car with New York tags make a U-turn on Sunrise and head west. The car had three guys in it and since I was a new cop I thought I'd better stop them for the U-turn, even though I should have had better things to do at that time of night.

The driver of the car saw my lights flashing, pulled to the right lane, hesitated, and then pulled over and stopped. As I stopped behind them I advised the dispatcher of what I was doing and heard her call for another unit to back me up.

The driver of the car, a young, tall latin-type with a lot of dark curly hair, got out of his car and came walking back to me. The other two sat in the car. I asked him for his driver's license and advised him of the U-turn violation and then went over to records channel to run the tag. As I was trying to decide whether or not to write the guy a ticket his two partners climbed out of the car and came walking back also. They were all standing around me like that when Russ, my zone partner, pulled up in his unit. He asked me which one was the driver and then pulled the other two away from me and had them stand with him by the trunk of their car while he checked their I.D.'s and ran their names through records.

I had decided to warn the driver and let them go when records came back and said the tag on the car was a "hit"... the car wasn't stolen, but was a current overdue rental from New York City. I asked the driver about it and he admitted that the car was rented but acted dumb about it being overdue. Russ heard what was going on and walked over to see the rental papers. As we followed the driver up the right side of the car Russ turned back and told me that overdues were a pain in the ass because once the rental company got their car back they rarely prosecuted, even though in many cases the "renters" had actually stolen the car, never intending to make any payments until they used it for their purposes, and then abandoning it somewhere.

The driver opened the right-side door and reached in and popped open the glove compartment. As he did so Russ unsnapped his holster, pulled his revolver out, and leaned in behind him, telling me out the side of his mouth to watch the other two. The driver stood up and handed Russ the papers, which were about two weeks out of date. Then he just stood there shrugging his shoulders. Russ looked at him a moment, then back at the other two, and said, "Check the car." Then he escorted the driver back to the rear of the car and had all three guys take up the position against the trunk.

I barely got my head in the door when I saw the first gun, a shiny automatic, lying on the floorboards almost under the seat on the right side. I said, "Russ..." and he said, "I know... keep looking," so I lifted a jacket lying on the seat and there was an old beat-up revolver. I grabbed it, found a big hunting knife under the driver's seat, and then looked in back. In a pocket of a peacoat lying on the floor was another revolver, and in a corner of the seat, stuffed into the crack, was a heavy set of brass knuckles.

Holy shit.

I backed out of the car and stared at the three guys leaning against the trunk, watching me. I had gone and found myself three honest-to-God-New-York-City-Latino-Puerto-Rican badasses in a stolen rental car, and they were mine, all mine.

I had all the guns and the knuckles and the knife stuffed in my pockets and my belt and I swaggered back to where Russ was standing behind the three guys and said, "Russ, these guys have this hot car and these guns, man, and they can only be here for one reason. They're gonna hit somethin' for sure," but Russ cut me off by saying, "Lock that stuff in the trunk of your cruiser, then get back here and pat these guys down." So I scurried back to my unit and dumped everything, trying to remember where each one was found for the report. Then I practically ran back up to Russ and the bad guys. Now records came back on the radio and advised they had a felony warrant on the driver, and there might be info on the other two but it would take a few minutes to confirm.

Well, I didn't have to wait a few minutes. Hell, I had these guys, guns, stolen car, felony warrant, and all. I brushed past Russ feeling pretty salty, and began to pat them down, one at a time.

The guy that had been in the back seat had a little .25 automatic in his pants, actually in his crotch. As I felt it he stiffened and Russ said quietly, "Don't even think about it, asshole," and I looked back to see Russ standing there with his old sort of rusty and tired-looking .38 revolver riding easily in his big hand, pointed past me at the latino's head. I managed to reach down into the guy's pants, past his balls, and wiggled the little gun out. I stuck it in my pocket and went to the next guy.

The second one started to turn when I got to him so I pushed him back and Russ said, "Cuff the first one and have him sit on the ground," so I pulled out my cuffs and did it and then went back to the second guy. He stood still this time while I pulled a hunting knife out of his belt at the small of his back. Even though I was moving fast, trying to make it look like I had thousands of body searches behind me, you know . . . being cool, I managed to feel something on the inside of his left leg, and lifting the pants I found a pearl-handled switchblade about twelve inches long in his sock.

I put his stuff away and turned and looked at Russ, who was still behind me and a little off to the side. This was in the days before those plastic throwaway "flexcuffs," so with Russ's cuffs we only had two sets for three dirtbags. Russ just said, "Have him sit on the ground too," and I did.

The last one for me to pat down was the driver, who looked over his shoulder at me and said, "Look, man, I'm not holdin' . . . you don't have to check me, I'm clean." I was feeling pretty smug, so I just said, "Right. turn around." I moved fast with him and tried to be careful but I didn't find anything until I got down to his soft leather boots with the high heels and the zipper up the back. I checked them both with my fingers and felt something hard in the left one. I unzipped it and there, squeezed in by his heel, was a pretty short-barrelled pearl-handled .22 revolver. I said, "Sure, you're clean," and pulled it out. I stuck it in my back pocket and said to Russ, "Gimme your cuffs." He used one hand to get them out of the case and hand them to me, and then watched as I cuffed the second guy's right hand to the driver's right hand. This is not as good as both hands behind the body, but it makes it very awkward and difficult for the two suspects to move in a coordinated manner . . . to run away.

I asked the dispatcher to send a wrecker to tow the car, and I stood the first guy up and walked him back to my unit, sitting him down in the back seat and closing the door. As I walked back to get the other two I had thoughts of how I would look as I drove these three hardcases to the jail door, as I drove through the sleeping streets of my city that I had

singlehandedly made safer by the apprehension of these pre-
dators.

I strutted up to the two handcuffed together and took the
driver by the arm to pull him toward my car, again with my
head filled with thoughts of telling the sergeant and the other
guys on my shift how I spotted these guys and how it went
down.

Russ said, "Wait. Wait a minute."

I stopped and so did the two guys and Russ moved behind
the driver, kneeled down, and with one hand started to pull
down the zipper on the back of the guy's right boot. I was just
going to tell him I had already checked it when another pretty
little short-barrelled pearl-handled .22 revolver, the twin to the
first one, fell into his hand. He looked up at me and I looked
at the driver, who just stared back at me evenly.

For a few seconds we were frozen there like that, and in those
seconds I stared into that driver's eyes and saw how he would
have used his one free hand to kill me, saw how I would have
looked with my brains spattered over the collar of my shirt, my
face twisted against the steering wheel, the blood running from
my open mouth into my lap. I could even see the headlines:
ROOKIE COP KILLED. I stepped back, still staring, and leaned
against the hood of my car. My legs felt weak and I thought I
might vomit.

I watched as Russ called for another unit, and as he did
another thorough search of all three guys again, making them
take off their shoes or boots, open their jackets, drop their pants.
When the other unit arrived Russ took that officer's handcuffs
and cuffed each guy behind his back. Then he stuffed them
into the back of the other officer's unit and asked him to run
them into jail for me.

I watched as the cruiser pulled away into the night, the three
figures sitting straight up in the back seat. I looked at Russ
standing quietly beside me and knew I had just had a whole
lot of cocky knocked right out of me. I knew Russ had just
given me another chance to learn, to survive. I looked at him

standing there, big and strong and confident, and I started to ask him how he knew.

He gave me a shrug and small smile and said, "They say the things you see on this job will kill you . . . but the ones you don't see will kill you sooner."

Six

ALMOST CHILD/WOMAN black girl standing across the street, watching me.

Her feet are bare in the hot fine powdery gray dirt. Her skinny legs already have several shiny black cut scars, knees white with dust, hands jammed into the hip pockets of her old sack dress (it has a high collar and a faded design of a bunch of balloons over the heart). Her hair is combed out natural, and I can see an imitation tortoise-shell pick sticking out of the back of it.

Her face is beautiful.

I doubt if she really knows how to apply makeup yet so she probably isn't wearing any. Even without it she is a classic. Diana Ross has come out to play street urchin.

So I'm doing my gig across the street, trying to jump-start this bill collector's car so he can get out of there in one piece, and she's standing there watching.

Probably just starting to get the idea that she's a woman, you know, feeling a little funny, seeing her breasts grow. I wonder if she has someone to tell her what it's all about, I wonder if she's dreamt of Prince Charming and all that stuff.

I look at her, and I know.

I know she won't even get a chance to be a little girl. I mean, you know she must think about growing up and meeting some guy who will treat her right, but will she know romance? Oh, I know that sounds stupid, but I'm worried that it's not fair. I mean, she's poor and she's black, and before she gets a chance to really dream about anything, fantasize about anything, some dude in a waxed, jacked-up '63 Chevy with a stereo and stolen mags is gonna come along and she's gonna see him strut and hear him talk and watch the muscles ripple under his skin, and hell, the next thing you know she's gonna be standing there across the street with a little black baby on her hip, with that old faraway expression in her eyes, and that almost child/ woman face.

Her face is beautiful.

I mean, will he take her to the Café de Paris? Will he order the Coq au Vin and just the right wine for her? Will she smile in the candlelight, knowing her earrings are sparkling just the way they should? Will the funny things she wants to say come out right? Will she get a chance to be nervous? Surprised? Can she walk down Las Olas Boulevard and window-shop with her lover, laughing at the ridiculous clothes in the windows and turning on the heel of her smart shoes?

I want her to be able to walk into the lounge on top of Pier 66, you know, very chic, very just so. I want her to be able to walk in there dressed to the nines with her hair shining and her back straight. I want her to be able to look around and know she's the best-looking lady there, escorted by the best-looking guy. I want her to look at the squads of blue-haired ladies and know that her evening dress costs twice as much as theirs, and that she knows how to wear it. I want the maitre d' to see her and her man as soon as they step off the elevator. I want him turning and snapping his fingers and bowing that little bow and just gliding along in front of them . . . taking them to the best seat in the place and seating them with a flourish.

I want her to feel the glow, to feel the love, the challenge, the excitement... to feel the quality of it all. Hell, I want her to enjoy the best part of being a beautiful woman. The subtle, intangible, quality stuff.

But I know.

Because I'm finished starting this clown's car and I'm walking back to my unit and I can see her standing there watching me, and I know.

She's an almost child/woman black girl.

And the odds are it's just not gonna happen.

Seven

SO HERE we go... out of the car and feet sliding in the gravel of the alley. There you are just roundin' the dumpster, one crushed-down sneaker comin' off while your feet grab for traction. I see you look over your shoulder, eyes wide, mouth open. You tryin' to be cool and run from me at the same time, asshole?

"Freeze, motherfucker, or I'll blow your face off!"

So you look over your shoulder again and turn right between the buildings, heading for the open field and the green apartments on the other side. You and I both know that when you get to those apartments you gonna disappear like a rat in a hole, huh? Well, guess again, asshole, cause there's my partner in the cruiser... waitin' for you.

"I said *stop*, asshole... I swear I'll blow you away!"

But you keep on runnin', turnin' again to get back into the alleys. Did you run this fast when you grabbed that old lady's purse? Did you have to knock her down and break her hip, you fucking dirtbag? Goddamn gunbelt weighs four thousand

pounds and bounces all over my hips . . . shit, I'm breathin' so
hard, you motherfucker, I'm gonna beat your ass.

Now! Now you slip right in front of me, don't you? Now you
roll and fall, and you look up at me with those big eyes. What
you coverin' your head for, boy? Cause you know I'm comin'
down, huh? *Yeah*. You so bad when you be takin' that old
woman's purse, you so bad when you be knockin' her down
and runnin' off like the wind. If you so bad how come a little
paddy motherfucker honky cop like me done got you down in
this alley? Huh? Why you be lookin' so helpless now, huh?
Why, motherfucker?

I stand over him, breathing hard. He's lookin' up at me with
those big wide eyes. His mouth is open, and when his shuddering breaths come out his lips quiver and the spit falls on his
chin. And he stinks . . . he stinks cause he's scared. I watch his
mouth as he looks up to say,

"Why you crackin' on me, man? I din' do nuthin', man. Why
you crackin' on me?"

And my fist impacts his face soooo hard it makes me want
to shout. I *do* shout, "Yeah motherfucker, let's see how bad you
really are!"

And I come down with the other fist. I'm gettin' good leverage
cause I'm standin' on the balls of my feet, puttin' everything
into it, left and right, my fists crunch into his face.

He screams, "*Nooooo*, man!" as his nose shatters and blood
flies everywhere.

With my right hand I grab him behind his sweaty head and
pull him up to his feet, "C'mon, you badass motherfucker!
C'mon, let's see, man!"

With my left I keep pounding his face, my fist crashing into
his mouth his eyes his throat, while he screams.

"I ain't bad, man! Oh *please* mister, I ain't bad!"

But you were so bad back there on the sidewalk, weren't you?
You *so* bad and you *so* cocky. Yeah, knock that old woman
down . . . old woman only lives a couple of blocks from you,
shithead. Knock her down and run off with her sorry little Social
Security check. Such a *bad* little motherfucker.

I lose my grip on his head and he falls to the gravel, bleedin' real good all over the place. As he sinks back I kick him once as hard as I can, one solid fucking kick right in his face. Blood and teeth fly and he rolls over into the dirt.

So here comes the sergeant and my partner, both sweating from running. I straighten up, clip my radio back onto my shirt and tuck my shirt back into my pants, dusting myself off as I do.

Sarge says, "What happened?"

Partner says, "You okay?"

I say, "Motherfucker fought with me, tried to take my gun, went for my throat... so I beat his ass."

Sarge looks down at the spitball, who is slowly trying to sit up. He says, "*Guilty*," and we stuff him into the back seat and drive out of the alley.

The people look. They say, "They hurt that boy."

Yeah.

We did. *I* did.

I did.

Eight

"WHY ARE you turning the car around? What did you see back there? We have dinner reservations for eight... we don't have time..."

"Wait a minute, honey, something didn't look right back there at that convenience store."

"Something didn't look right? So you have to turn around and go back, while we're supposed to be on our way to dinner?

You already did a shift today...you're *off duty* now!"

"Yeah, but somethin' just didn't look right...one dude by the side of the building, and the other hangin' by the phone..."

"So who are you, John Wayne? Can't you just leave it alone?"

"Well, dammit, they're gone now anyway. Must've just been looking the place over. Gee honey, don't get upset...I just had to take a look, that's all. They're gone, and we'll get on with the evening."

"But what if they'd still been there? You would have done ...what?"

"I don't know, watched them for a moment, that's all. They're gone, let's forget it, okay?"

Silence.

"You're supposed to leave the job at the station when you get off duty."

"Uh-huh."

"I don't want to play cops and robbers when we go out to dinner."

"All right."

"I want my husband to be a person all of the time, and a cop only some of the time. I feel like I don't even know you when you're a cop."

Silence.

Nine

"ALPHA TWO-THREE, make it code three, baby choking, not breathing. EMS also enroute."

I was on Commercial Boulevard, just west of Eighteenth Avenue when it came down, so I was just a short distance away. I stuffed the accelerator through the floor, made a wild sliding turn north through the intersection, and with my siren and lights going I headed for the address. Nothing gets a police officer going like a report of a child in trouble. All you want to do is get there, now, and fix whatever the problem is, now.

From several blocks away I could see a man standing in the middle of the avenue, waving his arms. I was glad to see it, it made finding the place that much easier. I figured it must be a neighbor helping the parents out. He moved out of the way as I roared up and slid into the parking lot. I popped the trunk with the button, jumped out, grabbed the oxygen, and went running toward the apartment. Three-A was standing open, and as I crashed inside I saw a young woman sitting on a sofa with her face buried in her hands, crying. The man who had been in the street was behind me. He had a terrified look on his face and pointed excitedly toward one of the rear rooms.

Baby's room. Winnie-the-Pooh and Garfield the cat. Blue sail-boats and yellow kites. Tiny T-shirts and miniature jogging shoes. Hopes and dreams and Ferris wheels.

I ran into the room and looked into the crib. There was the baby, around one year old, lying on his back in a little blue jumper. The muscles in his neck were stretched tight, and his face was a bright purple color. I threw the oxygen to the floor, thought about opening it and fooling with it, sensed the father (the man who had been in the street) looking at my back, stood up and grabbed the baby out of the crib and let its little head fall back against the back of my hand, opening its mouth.

His skin felt cool, but not dead cool.

I opened my mouth, covered his nose and mouth with it, and blew carefully. I did it again, and then again. Each time I did I watched the tiny chest rise and fall. Snoopy-the-dog and Mickey Mouse. Both parents were standing in the doorway behind me now, the father with a stricken look on his face and the mother with tears in her eyes, wringing her hands. A furry monkey from Grandma and a mobile made of little airplanes. Prayers and wishes and baseball caps.

I bent down and blew once more into the baby's nose and mouth. The baby hiccupped, struggled, gagged, turned pink, and started crying like you wouldn't believe, his small chest heaving as he took big shuddering gulps of air. He spit up on my shirt and grabbed my collar with his tiny hands. And he was breathing. And crying. And breathing.

I stood there with the EMS guys watching as the parents drove off with the baby to the hospital. Then I drove a few blocks away and sat on a park bench in the shade, drinking a lemonade.

It tasted great, and as I brought it to my lips I noticed that my hand was shaking pretty good.

Dad was standing in the street waving his arms around, and Mom was sitting on the sofa crying her eyes out while their hopes and dreams and wishes and prayers lay there turning purple. I shook my head.

After that baby started breathing again I should have put him back in his crib, turned around, and kicked his parents' asses.

Ten

I'M WAITING a couple of blocks away, out of sight in my marked patrol car because the tactical patrol officers don't want me to spook these three dudes they've been following around the south end. Tac has been watching these guys case places all night and they know it's only a matter of time before they rip something off.

The Tac sergeant comes on the radio and says the three suspects just drove their light blue Torino behind the wall of the service station at the corner of Andrews Avenue and State Road 84. He says they're getting ready to hit. I'm in an alley, my engine running, waiting. The sergeant comes back on and says it's goin' down. I'm still waiting to get the word to move in when the sergeant yells that they're running. Apparently some of the Tac guys tried to move in on 'em on foot, and the three bad guys jumped into the Torino and hauled ass out of the alley.

So when I hear this I pull out onto 84 and head east just in time to see a glimpse of the Torino sliding through the intersection southbound on Andrews . . . blue smoke everywhere. So here we go. I make my turn south on the avenue and I can see their taillights a block in front of me. They're really flying, a lot of smoke and sparks coming from the front of the car. They make a wild-ass left turn across the median a couple of blocks down and head for Federal Highway, but I'm closing in on them now and I can see the guy in the back seat turn and look at me. They turn south on Federal and I can hear a lot of yelling on the radio as the other units close in and I'm trying to tell the dispatcher where we are when the Torino hangs a right and cuts across Andrews again and then the railroad tracks and down into the industrial area . . . still flying.

I stay right with them and though I can't see any of the other units behind me I know the guys will be right with me any second. I follow behind as the Torino cuts back and forth across Second Avenue and finally makes a wild skidding left turn west on one of the side streets and heads down in between the big buildings there. I'm right on their ass as they skid across a big parking lot and run off the pavement into the scrub-brush filled ditch.

I'm screaming into the radio as I jump out and I watch as the doors fly open and the driver and passenger both jump out at once. The passenger is on the side of the Torino away from me so I just scream "*Freeze!*" and concentrate on the driver, who swings himself out hanging onto the door and then runs toward the front of the car and falls down. I run to the edge of the ditch and yell "*Freeze!*" again and he looks up at me with big eyes and turns to run. I've got my gun in my hand, but hell, the rules of the game say I can't shoot him and I guess he knows it so as he starts to move I hurl myself at him and land beside him with my right arm around his neck, trying to pull him down. At the same time I'm screaming, "*Hold it, asshole!*" and we both fall into the heavy underbrush. Apparently someone has been trimming trees and stuff because we are in a big pile of branches and limbs and sticks and things and it's just impossible to get any footing. As we fall I realize that this dude is no midget . . . probably six-three, two hundred and thirty pounds, big, round, and strong.

We struggle to get up and neither one of us can get to our feet but he's trying to pull away from me and we swap a couple of punches and I realize right away that this guy is gonna knock the shit out of me if I let him so I bring up my left hand with my revolver in it and I stick it right in his face and I scream, "*I'll fuckin' blow your head off!*" and he just says, "*Noooo!*" and grabs me in a bear hug and we roll down into the scrub again. The guy is big and strong and I'm struggling like a sonofabitch to get away from him and I'm hitting him behind the head with my right fist and I don't think he even feels it and I finally struggle to my knees and there we are, on our knees hugging each other, and he grabs the gun with both hands. When he does I haul back and hit him in the face with my right, solid, and as his face jerks back he keeps yelling, "No, no, no!" and pulling on the gun. His hands are very strong and even though I've got the gun solid by the grips I can feel him beginning to pull it away from me so I forget punching him in the face and grab at the gun with my right hand also.

So there we are, on our knees, face to face, chest to chest, with the gun in between, covered with our hands.

Now there is no screaming, just heavy breathing and grunting and I think he can smell my fear because he is getting stronger and starting to grin and I can feel his hands, like steel, slowly pulling my hands apart and I can see how it's gonna look and feel when this motherfucker gets my gun away from me and starts pumping 38s into my chest with my own gun and now I *am* getting scared and it's turning into a slow-burning, ass-tightening situation. With all my strength I try to pull the gun back closer to me and at the same time I'm trying to knee him in the balls but I can't get any power behind it and all I do is pull myself closer to him and now our faces are rubbing against each other and I can feel his greasy sweat and hear him breathing hard and grunting like an animal.

I know he's going to kill me.

At this point I decide it has to end. I can't let this fucker pull my gun away and shoot me and I can't pull away from him and control him and I still have my left hand on the grips of the gun with my finger on the trigger but I'm not really sure who has control of it. With all the twisting and turning I know the barrel is pointed up . . . up into our faces or chests, and I know when I pull the trigger the slug is gonna either rip up through the top of one of our skulls, or punch its way through one of our chests. Either way, it will be *me* doing it. He's grinning and pulling and I can feel my hands slipping and I know he's going to kill me and, fuck it, I'm gonna pull the trigger anyway and let the bullet blow away whichever one of us it hits. So I grab as tight as I can around the grips and get ready to jerk my head back hard before I pull the trigger, and I start to squeeze that motherfucker when suddenly I see this shiny black shoe *impact* the side of the guy's head and it jerks sideways and his eyes open wide and when he grunts his spit falls in my face but he still hangs onto the gun with his big hands and I'm still trying to pull back when the shiny black shoe gets him again, just above the left ear, and I hear a voice screaming, "*Die, you motherfucker!*" and as the guy turns his head toward the shoe it comes back and catches him right in the face, hard, just under the nose. Fucking blood and sweat and other shit smashes out all over me and I hear the guy groan and I feel his grip loosen. I pull hard and fall backwards into the tree limbs and see three guys jump into the ditch all over the guy and start beatin' the piss out of him. They're all screaming, "*Die! Die, motherfucker!*" and punching and kicking the crap out of him. I can hear him screaming and moaning but I just lay back and look up into the sky, breathing hard. I look down at my left hand and see the fingers wrapped around my revolver so tight that the skin is white.

I'm a little shaky but I slowly climb out from the tree limbs and crawl up out of the ditch and roll over and lay on my back in the parking lot, beside my cruiser. Finally I sit up and struggle to my feet. I'm a real mess. My uniform is ripped all over and I'm scratched and bleeding in a couple of places. I can still smell the guy's sweat on my face and I wipe my hands over it hard. Somebody asks, "You all right?" and I say, "Yeah," and lean against the car.

I watch as they drag the guy out of the ditch and throw him to the ground at my feet. His head is a bloody pulp, his mouth ripped open, and his eyes swollen shut. He is unconscious but breathing in ragged, chest-heaving gulps.

All the guys start grouping around me now and I hear them shouting and yelling, happy as shit because they recovered the money and all three suspects are *in custody*. The two guys that went out the passenger side of the Torino ran across a field and into another compound where they tried to hide in some trucks but the K-9 sniffed em' out and the dogs ate on both of em' and it's fucking beautiful.

I'm pulling my act together and I know we have to go sit around the emergency room while the night-shift doctor sews these assholes up before we can take them in for booking and the paperwork. I'm dusting myself off and Mike Gilant comes over and stands in front of me and I can see blood all over his right shoe and pants leg. He looks at me with a little smile and speaks quietly.

"You owe me one, Cherokee."

Eleven

I REMEMBER running as hard as I could through the soft yellow beach sand with the heavy resuscitator swinging unevenly in my right hand. I was running against death, and I was awkward and scared, and when the metal edge of the resuscitator crashed against my leg I almost fell into the sand.

I was already sweating from the exertion and blazing sun when I reached the water's edge where the small group of people were crowded uncertainly around the young boy lying sprawled on his back in the wet sand. One woman, his mother, was kneeling beside his slim pale form, and as I threw myself down beside him she looked up at me and pleaded a silent piercing scream with her eyes.

Half of the boy's face was covered with wet sand, and his hair was wet and plastered against his head. His chest made uneven convulsions, and his hands fluttered several times as if he were trying to stop his life from escaping his small body. His eyes had that half closed staring, clouded look, and his lips were bright purple. His head was turned slightly and the lower edge of his mouth and his chin were slick-wet with what he had thrown up.

While I ripped open the snaps on the lid of the green metal box with one hand I wiped my other hand roughly across the little mouth, grabbed the back of his head by the hair and pulled his head back so his mouth gaped open, brought my hand back and pinched his nose, and placed my mouth over his. I blew as hard as I could into his mouth but my lips slid away from his and most of the air made an obscene sound as it rushed around between our faces. I was still fumbling with the parts of the resuscitator with one hand while I held his head with the other. I knew I could pump air into him mouth-to-mouth, and if I could get the resuscitator going I could force pure oxygen into his system. I knew other officers were coming to me as backup, and that lifeguards would be on their way from the other parts of the beach. If only I had some help *now*.

I was on my knees in the wet sand, pants wet with saltwater and shoes buried up to the laces. The hot sun beat down and the people grouped around watching and the sweat ran into my eyes and burned and the little chest heaved again and as I pulled the hose out of the box and grabbed the valve handle I again blew into the wet mouth and this time saw the chest move as I did. I looked up quickly to reach for the small face-piece in the top of the green box and as I did the mother's eyes burned into mine and she crashed into my concentration with her single burning sob. With that sob she asked, *will he live will he be alright will you save my little boy*, and I tore my eyes away from hers already knowing the horrible answer in my heart and hating it.

Hating it.

Seconds were flashing by and I was still breathing into the little mouth and holding his head back and letting go of his nose long enough to fit the facepiece onto the end of the green rubber tube and breathing again and trying to fit the valve handle to the stud and the sweat was in my eyes and the people standing around pushed closer and a roar began to fill my head as the whole scene compacted into my parched mouth on his, my leaden, paralyzed hands working against the cold steel equipment, the little chest breaking its stillness with ragged heaves... and the burning eyes of the boy's mother, pulling at me, reaching for me, wanting me to tell her that the nightmare would end soon and the picnic could resume. As I went on bending and reaching and breathing and working I found my mind separating itself from my body. I was able to pull away and observe the agonizing tableau in hypnotic silence. I could see the dark brown shirt plastered against my back, and the veins at my temples stand out as I forced the air into the little body. I could see the silver watch on the reddened wrist of the mother as she clutched her hands against her face. I could see the small white feet spread against the packed sand, each sparkling grain was like a jewel against his skin. I watched mesmerized as one of the fluttering hands reached out and grabbed the gray cloth of my trouser leg and began twisting it gently. Time did not stop, but moved around us, leaving us there on the beach in the searing sun. It washed against us, broke at our backs, and rushed by, pulling at our conciousness as it did.

Suddenly a commotion began and I looked up to see other officers and two lifeguards. Strong hands grabbed for equipment and strong voices pushed back the people grouped around. The facepiece was fitted against the boy's face and pure oxygen forced into him. The lifeguards and other officers were all grouped around the boy now and I sat back on my heels, looked up into the sky, and took several deep breaths. As I wiped off my face I looked at the mother. Her eyes had left me now and were turned toward her little boy, and she watched as the other men tried to capture his small life and fit it back into his body. When the ambulance arrived and the boy was lifted and placed onto the stretcher, still surrounded by the officers and lifeguards, she stood with them, and still clutching one hand she ran beside them as they hurried as best they could through the soft sand toward the ambulance.

I stayed on my knees in the sand as the noise of the siren faded away and the crowd reluctantly separated and let the scene pass away into their memories. I felt numb as I stood and collected my equipment and tried to brush the clinging sand from my pants. As I trudged slowly back up the beach to my car, the heavy metal box bumping my leg, I heard someone say, "Eleven."

He was eleven.

I cried later when the emergency room nurse told me he would live. Yes, he would live and I broke down and looked at the white tiles on the floor and cried. I cried as a release and in relief and because the boy had been saved. Had I known I was crying in response to a cruel joke played on us all I would have turned my face up to Him in anger and agony and confusion.

I left there that day ignorant of the cruel joke and went home believing that the boy had been saved. He would live. Yes, he would live.

Several months later I pulled my unit up into the emergency room breezeway and got out to use the telephone. As I did I saw the automatic glass doors at the entrance slide open, and with a hydraulic hiss the joke was exposed.

A man, he could have only been the father, was carrying the boy in his arms. The dangling legs swung easily and the feet were pointed in and the toes bumped against each other. The slender arms hung limply and the delicate hands fluttered uncontrollably. His head hung back, away from his father's strong shoulder. His mouth was open, and his questioning eyes stared up into the sky. I don't know if his eyes saw the sun. His soft brown hair was clean now and waved against his pale forehead. The mother walked along beside him, still clutching one of her son's hands. As they walked by she turned and looked at me but her eyes did not see me and this time they asked me no questions. She knew the answer now, just as I did so many months ago on that unforgiving beach.

No woman. Your child will not *live*. He will breathe and eat and soil himself... but he will not have a *life*. Her head turned and the eyes slid off me and looked off into whatever future she was given.

I turned around, confused, not knowing why I was there. I wanted to strike out, to grab the one responsible and crush His throat with my hands. The rage and pain were like molten lava in my heart and I wanted to curse Him and let my fists crash against his face in a never-ending barrage.

Instead I looked up into the sun, numb from the pain and confusion, and felt the tears forming.

But *no*.

I wouldn't. *I could not cry.* And I wouldn't.

Twelve

"HONEY, YOU look tired, or down, or something. Was it a tough day?"

"Yeah. It's already been a tough month this week. Had a near-drowning today, and..."

"They had you out on the beach? I thought you worked the southend... how long are they going to keep moving you around just because you're new?"

"The beach is sort of part of the southend... anyway, this kid..."

"Johnny's wife told me you guys like to work the beach so

you can sit at East Las Olas and A-I-A and watch the little
college girls in their bikinis. She said you guys all wear your
sunglasses and stand around with your arms folded, looking
macho."

"The beach is a pain in the ass. Everybody's daddy is a
lawyer."

"You should hear how tight your voice is now. Ease up,
honey, I'm just asking."

"Yeah. I'll tell you something, I'd rather work friggin' blacktown than the beach. You wouldn't believe the maggots and
dirtbags out there ... no matter how hard you try to be civil or
decent with them, half the time you wind up kicking their ass
anyway."

"'Blacktown?' Why does there have to be a distinction? Why
are they separate in your mind from the people on the beach?
And why do you always revert to the physical ... can't problems
be handled any other way?"

"It's not that ..."

"One of my professors said today: 'Problem-solving through
the use of physical violence is usually the result of a mind
frustrated by its own inability to discern various avenues of
communication.' In other words, honey, 'kicking ass' is the easy
way, because you can't figure out any other solution when
dealing with a problem."

"Gosh, you must have some pretty smart teachers out there
at Broward Community College ... feeding you such meaningless bullshit."

"It's not meaningless. Every time you come home from that
job ... you should hear your words, all the time kicking somebody's butt, or choking them out, or whatever. It bothers me.
Out there on that campus people use their minds to solve problems, not their fists."

"Some problems are theoretical and can be solved with pro-
found thoughts, some are immediate and real ... and these
sometimes require a more physical approach."

"Oh, nonsense. Appreciation and examination of theory gives
you a headstart on dealing with reality."

"Sheesh."

Pause.

"Well, what about you, lady, how was your day?"

"I *learned* today, while you kicked ass."

"Goddamn it . . ."

My wife was now in college full time, she loved it and did well. She became involved with a new social circle and activities. She was fast becoming as comfortable in her world as I was in mine. There began a subtle, unperceived drift apart. The obvious things glared at us, like my irritating her at restaurants by always wanting to sit with my back to the wall so my eyes could watch the front door and the cash register, and her backing of some political candidate I had pegged as a hopeless liberal ineffective do-gooder. We didn't pick up on the deceptive ones, like which sections of the newspaper we went for on Sunday mornings, or which television shows we enjoyed, or which books we brought home (Joseph Wambaugh and Mack Bolan, Dr. Wayne Dyer and Hunter Thompson). It was in the way I stacked groceries and slammed doors, the way she rigidly controlled the budget and constantly described our financial limitations. I became the aggressor in our lovemaking, occasionally and unwittingly demanding, and unaware that much of my gentleness had been replaced with an almost territorial urgency. She became the "gift-giver" in our lovemaking, maintaining an emotional distance even when there was no physical distance at all.

We were academia and asphalt, and we could not escape the subtle effects of our dichotomous perceived realities.

Thirteen

So WOODLARK says, "Pull in here, under that big oak, and we can eat these burgers and relax for a couple of minutes."

So I do, and as I back the cruiser into the shade we see an old wino sacked out on a ruined car seat near the base of the tree.

"Shit."

"Yeah... well, let's eat anyway. I don't feel like messin' with him."

I shut her down and we open the car doors and sit back, one foot on the dash, tellin' war stories and eating greasy burgers. We're talking about sex and some of the kinky ladies we've heard about and exchanging information we've picked up about various dispatchers and their many talents and shit like that, you know, and once in a while I look back to see if the wino is gonna get up and come over and try to scrounge some change or somethin' but he ain't moving so I'm back to the burgers and tall tales and Woodlark's lightin' up a smoke and I'm trying to burp as loud as I can and we're kinda laying back when the dispatcher comes on and wants to know our location, you know?

So Woodlark grabs the mike and says, "Yeah, Bravo Forty-four. We're ten-six at Northwest Sixth Street and Seventh Avenue checkin' out a deuce who don't look too good."

We both smile when she gives the call to Smith and Dunphy over in Bravo Forty-two.

Then, since we said we were, we got out and walked back

to the old wino still sacked out on the car seat and I kick his feet and say, "Hey, you old smelly shit...drop your cock and grab your socks, it's time to rise and shine," but when I do a huge cloud of big blue bottle flies comes buzzin' up from around his face and Woodlark says, "Shit," and grabs the back of the car seat and gives it a jerk and the old wino just rolls right over and falls onto the asphalt.

Man...his face was just as purple as could be...mouth open and all foamy and he was stiff as hell. His hands, they had been under him when he was layin' face down on the seat, were gripping his crotch, hard, and his pants were all wet and then the smell really came up and caught me and I threw up all over my shoes and the trunk of the cruiser.

Woodlark laughed and talked on the radio for a moment and said, "Asshole died with his hands in his pants...then he lays there and stinks while we eat our lunch. If he didn't smell so bad I'd put him in the back of the car and take him in and book the sonofabitch."

"For what?" I say.

And Woodlark says, "Obstructing Fucking Justice."

Fourteen

ONE OF the local big-time private defense attorneys had been around so long and had such a reputation for making cops look foolish in court, that just his name was enough to cause concern among the younger police officers discussing court activities.

I called this particular attorney Howdy-Doody because he had

red-blond hair (always well and expensively styled), a speckled
tan complexion, thick lips, and puffy cheeks. He tried hard to
be fashionable, but time and gravity and various recreational
narcotics had taken their toll and he had that apple-that-sat-in-
the-sun look, know what I mean? To me he looked like a tired
old man trying to go to a party as Howdy Doody, except that
the real Howdy Doody character was one of decency and fairness and wholesomeness and many other good things that we
all looked up to when we were kids. This guy was none of those
things.

Legend had it that long ago, when Howdy was a young and
new attorney, he had been arrested and beaten by one of the
older cops, and then beaten again in court when it came to
trial. Since that time, legend said, Howdy hated all cops and
would go out of his way to hurt one in court or during trial if
he could. He not only handled the defense for criminal cases,
he was always active in the civil end of it, right there encour-
aging clients to sue some cop. Working a lawsuit against a
municipality is not difficult to manage. Money can be made
just by writing a letter advising the city attorney that a lawsuit
is eminent. Many times the city will settle with a quick sum of
money rather than go through a lengthy, costly court battle.
This means that no one really cares about the validity of the
cop's arrest.

Was the cop right in his actions? Who cares?

Anyway, this Howdy Doody was very much like a circling
buzzard in a three-piece suit (but never a tie—a chain maybe,
or a medallion, but never a tie). The fashionably flamboyant
carrion-eater.

I had been a cop for about three years when Howdy presented
this story to the court in a lawsuit against me, two other cops,
and the city:

His client, a woman in her late forties, had been lying in her
bedroom, in her house, on her bed, peacefully, when three
Gestapo-psychotic-sadistic-rights-disdaining cops smashed in
her front door, pushed her elderly husband around, threatened

her innocently charming son, and charged into her bedroom to arrest her *for no reason*. They beat her and dragged her from the house, and when she attempted to reason with them they cursed at her and humiliated her and beat her some more. They dragged her onto the street, in front of the neighbors, and forced her into a police car, breaking her toe in the process. All the way to jail she was cursed at and publicly humiliated, and once there the monster jailers removed her upper denture and smashed it so she couldn't eat anymore.

This was the tale Howdy presented to the jury in a three-day trial. I don't want to bore you with the facts, like the whole neighborhood called the police because of a disturbance and the police responded three different times. Like the old husband asked us to protect him from his wife, like the son was a felon, like the woman was a violent mental whose shrieking, filthy screams made people bring their children inside. Like the police gave her warning after warning but finally had to take her away, fighting violently and injuring all three officers with minor cuts and scratches.

Like how she took her upper denture out of her mouth and smashed it repeatedly against the holding-tank window until it finally broke.

Let me just say that the official police version of the incident was was a wee bit different than Howdy's.

Anyway, during my time as a cop I had gone up against Howdy three times in court. In each case he worked real hard to get his client off the charges by making my life extremely difficult on the witness stand. Attorneys can play many games with a cop on the stand, they can say things to him they would never say outside of the judicial womb. Most attorneys fight very hard for their clients, and will vigorously attack a cop's testimony on the stand. That's the way it should be. Some attorneys, however, get dirty about it. They like to try to humiliate the cop, or make him look stupid, or crooked, or incompetent, or all of these things. They will get personal or out-of-line in their questioning, and unless the prosecutor or the judge makes an effort to curb this the cop can take a beating. In each case where I had arrested Howdy's client he fought dirty in court, and in every case his client had been found guilty anyway.

Howdy didn't like me.

The jury sat through three days of the story of the poor woman being dragged from her bed. They heard from the son, the cops, the mind and body doctors, and from the attorneys for both sides. On the last day during closing arguments Howdy got really dramatic. As he begged for the jury to find for his client and against the police, thus making the streets safer and cleaner for everyone and proving to the police that the public would not tolerate such Nazi nonsense, he threw himself to his knees in front of the jury box. It was pretty impressive. He had his hands clasped in front of his chest and his puffy face fixed into an expression of pain, while behind him his client sat dabbing her stricken, weeping eyes. All we needed was a violin section behind the judge and naked cherubs throwing rose petals around the room.

After that performance we all trooped out into the hallway to await the jury's decision. While I stood there with my hands in my pockets Howdy walked up to me, gave me a sneer, and said, "Well, how do you feel *now?*" Then he turned and walked back to his client. The answer was I felt like a lump of dogshit, but I don't think I could have explained it to him anyway. I guess he was pumped up about having been in combat with me and my partners. He had challenged his adversaries, had been in a conflict situation, and probably felt it was very real. I knew I could never make him understand that his proud arena was a cesspool of falsehoods, facades, deception, and dishonor to me. The combat I waged in *my* arena was so real it stung your eyes, and I knew I would never have the chance to face him or his kind there.

A short time later the jury came back and we all stood there as they told us they found against the woman and Howdy, and for the city.

We were exonerated of any wrongdoing.

Hurrah.

I had other business in the courthouse so it was a short time later that I pushed into a crowded elevator to get out of there and go meet the other guys for a celebratory sandwich. Standing next to me was one of the jurors from my case. She was an elderly woman, a real grandmotherly type, with little white curls and a print dress. She had a sweet face and nice smile, and I said to her, "Whew... I'm sure glad that's all over."

She smiled and patted my arm and said quietly, "Yes, you and those other boys really went through the wringer on that one, didn't you? Well, never mind."

I said, "Thank you," and she had a twinkle in her eye as she went on, "You know, officer, I tried through that whole trial to keep an open mind and listen to the testimony so I could be fair in my decision. Even at the end I was prepared to go into the jury room and consider the whole case fairly. But when that asshole got down on his knees in front of me I *knew* he was lying... and that was that."

She smiled again and clutched her purse to her side as she stepped off the elevator and walked away.

Fifteen

THE OLD Davie Boulevard drive-in was like any other drive-in movie lot anywhere. The big screen, which was missing several panels, was located in the northwest corner of the property. In the middle was the blockhouse that had been the combination projection building and snack bar. It was a boarded-up square of whitewashed concrete now. The rest of the lot was empty tarmac expanse, except it had row after row of crescent-shaped mounds that curved from one end of the lot to the other. On top of the mounds were rows of holes where the sound poles used to be. The best part about the old lot, and the part that made it the favorite hangout for guys who had to do paperwork, or who wanted to have a quiet cup of coffee without being distracted by the paying public, was that the whole place was surrounded by giant Australian pine trees. The trees had been planted years ago to keep nonpaying persons from watching silent movies from a distance. The trees now made it possible for three or four police units to be in there at the same time without being seen by the traffic on Davie Boulevard or the residents who lived in the houses that surrounded the lot.

I was working the West Fifties on day shift with John and Frankie covering the other nearby zones. Often during day shift things were slow, so we would go looking for trouble, checking the bad neighborhoods, the usual stolen car drops, places where the dirtbags hung out, stuff like that. We were supposed to be three separate units working our zones but we always backed each other, so if one of us found something to work the others would show up anyway so usually we made a three-car caravan everywhere we went.

John looked more like a high school kid than a cop. He had sandy blond hair and a fair complexion and a little-boy face that made women just want to hug him to their breasts. He was smart as a whip and had a razor wit, and he loved pranks and tricks. And he was good at it. He had married his highschool sweetheart and was consumed by her. He played it straight with the ladies and was respected by the other guys because he didn't back down when the shit hit the fan.

Frankie was from Jersey. He was an Italian but had dark skin and almost afro hair that made him look latin. In fact, a lot of blacks used to describe him as that "bright-skinned brother," which infuriated him and gave John and me more ammo to zing him with. He had recently married a woman who already had kids and he was working hard and playing it straight. He was a fighter, and had an explosive temper, and woe be unto the street maggot that messed with him.

It was day shift, the middle of a hot and clear summer, and the three of us were out there wired for sound and ready to boogie.

The last character in this deal was one Lonnie D. Spooner. Spooner was a dirtbag. A maggot. A soilsack, greaseball, shithead, spitball, and just plain rotten puke. Even worse than that, Lonnie D. Spooner was an Asshole. Let me put it this way: most dirtbags and maggots thought Spooner was a dirtbag and a maggot.

Spooner was tall and gangly, all elbows and knees. He had big knuckly hands and he slouched when he walked. His hair was greasy black and hung in limp strings from the top of his pointed skull. This guy was ugly, like a cross between Frankenstein's alter ego and Quasimodo. As an artistic touch he had white skin with thick loose wet purple lips, accented by heavy eyebrows and wild acne. What a beauty.

Don't get me wrong. Spooner wasn't a dirtbag simply because he was ugly. Most cops can forgive ugly, but no cop can forgive child molesting. Spooner wasn't just ugly, he was dangerous. He had a history of burglary, business and residential, and car theft was something he had dabbled in but was too technical for him. He would have been one more dirtbag burglar if it wasn't for that quirk of his.

He liked to hang around girl's bathrooms.

He preferred elementary school girls, with their pink dresses and shiny black-buckle shoes and clean white socks just above the ankle. Once he had been caught drilling a hole in the wall between the boys' room and the girls' so he could look in on them. He had been chased out of bathrooms on several school grounds many times, and his activities had been reported to the police. Under juvenile law he had once, years ago, been turned over to a "counselor" for help and guidance after being convicted of molesting a little girl. It had no effect on him, and during the summer of this tale Spooner was out sliming around on the streets.

It was the middle of the day and things were slow and John and Frankie and I were behind the Mormon church under the trees shooting the breeze when a call came out that a "strange white male" was on the grounds at Sunset Elementary School. As we headed that way the dispatcher gave a description and right away we knew who it was. We'd talked about Spooner many times, and would have loved to have caught him in the act so we could blow him away without too much of a stink.

As we got into the area, sure enough, Spooner could be seen loping off across the playing field. John headed for the school office and Frankie and I circled around the block in time to see that scraggly maggot jump a low fence and come running onto a sidestreet. We roared up on him and stopped and he stood there with his hands in the air like he was a heavy dude. We patted him down and Frankie asked him what he was doing on the school grounds. Spooner denied being there. Frankie asked him why he was running from us then, and he said he had been jogging.

With this Frankie took off like a rocket. He grabbed the front of Spooner's shirt, tearing it, and screamed in Spooner's face, "Hey, *shithead*... who the *fuck* you think you're jivin' here?" He threw Spooner against the hood of the cruiser, and Spooner turned his head and spit on the ground.

John arrived then, pulled us aside, and told us Spooner had been hanging around the school grounds for about a half hour and the staff just wanted him shooed away. Frankie told John about the jogging and John smiled and said to Spooner, "Why, Mr. Spooner, how positively athletic of you. Jogging in this heat? My... you must be dedicated. The problem is the staff at the school told me you've been hovering about in your devious and perverted way, and guess who we're going to believe?" Spooner looked down at his feet and said, "I didn't do nuthin', man."

I had run Spooner's name through records and learned there were no active warrants on him so we knew there was nothing we could do with him this time. He wasn't holding any dope or weapons, and if the school staff wouldn't press charges he was going to walk. Frankie was still hot so he got back in

Spooner's face and said, "Looks like you slide this time, dipstick, but if I ever catch you around that school again I'll kick your slimy ass!"

Spooner looked at him and said again through a little grin, "I didn't do nuthin', man."

The three of us exchanged looks, shook our heads, and turned to get back into out units to leave, and Spooner blurted out, "But what about my shirt? This cop tore my shirt..." We all stopped and turned on him but Frankie got there first and said quietly, "Stuff the shirt up your ass. Now... get out of here before I decide to do it for you." Spooner put his hands up in front of his face and said, "Okay man, forget it," so we all turned away again thinking that was the end of it but for some reason Spooner just couldn't let it go, and he pointed a bony finger at Frankie and croaked, "*Hey*... I know where you live, cop!"

We all froze and slowly turned to face Spooner, who was standing in the street, eyes wide, licking his lips. No one spoke but I could tell that John, like me, was thinking of the small home a couple of blocks from the pistol range, and of the kids playing in the yard, and of Frankie's wife coming home with a carload of groceries. We looked at Frankie and saw that he was seeing the picture with Spooner in it. Spooner near his kids, in his house, looking at his wife. John just barely got to Frankie and grabbed the back of his wide leather gunbelt before Frankie launched himself with a guttural snarl. Spooner turned to run, but I was on him too quick, my own anger snapping like a rubber band. I popped him a couple of times on the side of the head and herded him back against my unit, where he leaned back across the trunk, cowering under his long arms. Frankie was dragging John toward Spooner, his right arm cocked back and loaded with a tight fist, and John hissed in his ear, "*No, Frank! Not here, man!*"

"Let's just book this asshole for threats to a police officer," I said. Frankie said, "Book him? Shit." John said, "Load him into your unit and follow me." He got close to Spooner's sweaty face then, and said quietly, "You're going to love this, Spooner." Spooner looked around wildly and asked, "What are you gonna do to me?" John smiled his angellic smile and whispered, "We're going to *execute* you, motherfucker."

We pushed Spooner into the back seat of my unit and slammed the door. Then we looked at each other, each one searching out what was behind the other's eyes. None of us was disappointed. No matter how far this game went we would all keep playing.

As I followed the other two units toward the old Davie drive-in lot Spooner sat in the back seat and went through several changes. First he was enraged, screaming, "Motherfucker!" and crashing his forehead against the Plexiglass shield behind my head. Then he lay down on the seat and tried to kick out the back windows, so I slammed on the brakes, which caused him to impact the shield again, and then he began pleading with me. "C'mon man. Just let me go. I'll go away man, I've got people up north... I'll split and you guys will never see me again." Then he sat back there and snuffled.

I followed my partners' units into the movie lot and pulled up beside them near the blockhouse in the center. Spooner was quiet now and watched wide-eyed as we got out of our cars and stood looking into the rear window at him. John was the first to speak. "Now it won't do you any good at all to know where my partner lives, will it?" He opened the door and reached inside. Spooner pulled back against the other door and through clenched teeth said, "Man, I didn't do *nuthin!*... and you can't *do* this!" Frankie jerked open the other door and Spooner almost fell out but slid into the middle of the seat and sat there huddled with his knees in his face. Frankie reached in and grabbed one skinny arm and said tightly, "Now you gonna be a badass? You gonna come round my house? No... cause you're gonna be *dead!*" He dragged Spooner out and dumped him on the pavement, and we watched as Spooner struggled to his feet and stood there staring at each of us, disbelief and fear in his eyes. I turned him around and took off the handcuffs I had locked on him before he went into my car, and as he massaged his wrists Frankie said, "Now let's see how bad you are, man. You going to be bad at my house? Show me now what you gonna do there..." Spooner tried to back away but hit the car and then leaned back, his hands in front of his face. Frankie was on the balls of his feet, fists clenched into hammers, seconds away from jumping...

The electric pause was broken by John, who said easily, "Hold it, Frankie. Hold on a moment." Frankie turned his head slightly and asked quietly, "What did you do that for?" and John touched him on the arm and winked and said, "Well, like the witch in *The Wizard of Oz* said, these things must be handled delicately ... you know?" We all looked at him, and he went on, "We don't want to get jammed up over wasting this bag of puke, do we? Do you want to dig his I.D. out of his filthy pockets after we shoot him? Even though he's a scroat, if they find I.D. on him there could be a serious follow-up investigation, and there might be trouble, see what I mean?" He winked again and I could see Frankie relax so I said, "Let's make sure this scum is clean *before* we execute him." Spooner licked his lips and said unevenly, "Hey... really you guys... you're not gonna kill me, right? I was just kidding about your house, officer..."

This just set Frankie off again and he grabbed Spooner's already torn shirt and lifted his skinny frame up so Spooner's face hung over his and he said, "That's it... time to die, asshole!" Again John broke the mood by saying in a disapproving voice, "Put him down, Frank, he's got work to do over here." John walked over beside the blockhouse where there was a strip of dirt and gravel and a few tufts of tenacious weed. He pointed at the dirt and told Spooner to get over there and empty his pockets. Spooner froze for a moment, then stumbled to the blockhouse. He kneeled down and tentatively dug a few handfuls of dirt, then stopped and looked up at us and shook his head. All three of us reached for our holsters and at the same time all three snaps were popped open and our hands were resting on the grips of our service revolvers. Spooner giggled, then sobbed, and quickly emptied his pockets... his wallet, some change, a bent comb, and some papers. He held onto the papers for a moment, then dropped them, and Frankie bent down and picked them up and unfolded them. They were two pages from a catalogue, pages showing little girls in pretty dresses, and little girls in pajamas. Frankie let the papers flutter to the ground, pulled his weapon out of the holster, held it down by his leg, and said through his teeth, "Dig... motherfucker."

Spooner sobbed again, dug some more, then placed all the stuff in the hole, covered it over, and stood up shakily, saying, "Oh, please don't do this to me, you guys."

Frankie stepped closer to him, brought his weapon up, and pushed it under Spooner's nose. We all held our breath for a moment, watching the muscles in Frankie's forearm ripple, and the skin across his knuckles turn white with the tension. It was close, real close.

"Hey, guys, this isn't going to work at all," said John, his timing perfect as usual. The glimmer of hope that crossed Spooner's face clouded over as John continued, "My cleaning bill is already too high, and when Frankie pulls that trigger all the dead lizards and other shit that is packed into Spooner's skull is going to splatter all over us. Much too messy. We've got to do this without looking like we've been to a pig-skinning festival." Frankie grinned and that was a good sign, and John went on, "Let's make it sporting. Let's give this dirtbag a chance to run for his life."

Spooner was staring at Frankie's revolver in his face, and gulped. John folded his arms across his chest, thumbs up, and said, "We let Spooner run across two mounds in any direction ... a little head start... and then we jump into our units and give chase. The object is to gun him down on the run, but we have to be sitting in our cars to do it, and no running him over either. That wouldn't be fair, and besides, if we hit him with a car we'd have to hose off the front end with Lysol." We nooded grimly and looked at Spooner, who stared back dumbfounded. "What's the matter, Spooner?" asked John, "Didn't you hear me? All you have to do is run like hell and make it to the trees and you're free... until the next time we see you. *If* you make it to the trees you should remember that somewhere out here in this world there are three *absolutely* psycho cops looking for you. Got it?"

With that he turned toward his unit and yelled, "*All right!* Let's get his ass!" Frankie and I fell all over ourselves trying to get to our cars, and Spooner stood there for a few seconds and then screamed, "*No fair!* I'm supposed to get a head start..." Then he turned and began running as fast as he could across the lot toward the pine trees along the west perimeter.

With revving engines and screeching tires we took off after him and it was wild from the start. The parking mounds were just high enough so that if you hit them at speed the car would fly through the air and crash down into the flat area in between. I watched as John's car skidded violently near Spooner, who fell to the ground and rolled, then staggered up and began running again. I came over the mounds too fast, almost lost control, and went screaming by him with my gun in my left hand. He saw me coming and fell to the ground with his hands over his head. I looked in the rearview mirror to see him get up and turn in a full circle before starting off toward the trees in an uneven lope. I looked around as I put my weapon back in its holster and saw that neither John nor Frankie had theirs out. I felt relieved.

After a few more passes, with Spooner trying to evade us like a matador on Quaaludes, John and I brought our units to a stop back over by the blockhouse. We watched as Frankie gunned his engine and pulled his car around in a wild sliding turn and headed back toward the stumbling figure. Frankie's car approached from directly behind Spooner, who had only about twenty-five yards to the trees now. Instead of hitting the mound at an angle Frankie's car hit it almost straight on. Its speed caused it to leap up into the air and from where John and I were sitting it looked like the car would land right on top of Spooner. I said, "Shit," as the car came crashing down onto the pavement and then skidded sideways. Spooner was not visible.

Then the police unit moved forward slightly and we could see Spooner on his hands and knees crawling like mad into the scrub around the base of the pines. All that was visible was his bony rear end, his feet, and his elbows sticking into the air. Dust flew up as he shuffled his way through the pine needles. Frankie got out of his unit, jumped onto the hood, and yelled, "*Goodbye, you slimy motherfucker!*"

When Frankie drove back to the blockhouse and parked beside John and I we just sat there a moment, smiling. Then we drove slowly out of the drive-in and back on the prowl.

Recently I was out on Davie Boulevard and I passed where the old drive-in used to be. The whole area was bulldozed some years ago and now there is a big shopping center there. I thought about the incident with Spooner, and remembered that we never did see him again.

I smiled.

May his personal effects rest in peace.

Sixteen

IT WAS early afternoon when she made her decision. By the time the fierce red afternoon sun penetrated the green wall of twisting vines and hanging plants on her porch its rays were barely able to turn the inside of her living room a soft golden bronze. The velvet shadows hung on the edges of her old-style furniture and only the occasional chirping of a bird interrupted the steady rhythm of the grandfather clock standing against the far wall.

Once she made up her mind she felt better and knew she had to get busy to prepare for her guests. She knew how to entertain... why, she could tell you such stories about when she was a little girl and all the excitement a gentleman caller would bring. Oh, no time for that now, she really must get ready.

She combed her gray hair out and then fixed it in a nice tight bun on the top of her head. She put a small silver comb in it for just that touch, you know. Then she put on her long purple dress, the one with the round embroidered collar and thin belt. Very carefully she put on a small amount of makeup . . . not too much, the soft light in the room had always been kind to her, she thought. Of course there was the time when she did not need any makeup even in the harsh light of a sunny day . . . but that was so long ago, and really, there was still so much to do.

She straightened up the living room but of course everything was in its place and as neat as a pin as always so she went into the kitchen to check on the sweetness of the lemonade she had made earlier. She liked it tart, but she had to consider her guests' tastes too, so she added a pinch of sugar. Perfect. Then she got out the tin of butter cookies she kept on top of the refrigerator. She put several out on a tray, got out two of her nice crystal goblets, and was ready.

She looked around the house again to make sure all was in order, checked herself in the full-length mirror in her bedroom, closed that door, went into the hallway, and called the police.

As she sat in the living room shadows she thought how brusk and efficient that young woman had sounded on the telephone. So masterful. My, the young ladies of today certainly were no shrinking violets, were they?

After a few minutes she heard the car pull into her driveway and she stood quietly until the chimes rang, hesitated just a second, and then opened the door. There, standing on the front porch, were two young police officers. Both stood very straight, she noticed, and she thought that was nice . . . and they both had mustaches, and that was nice too. Remember when all the young men had mustaches and they fussed with them so, always waxing them and having them trimmed? But really, no time for that now, the young officers must be thirsty.

So she bade them come in and as they did they both took off their hats, which she thought was the perfectly natural thing for them to do, and then she asked them to please sit down and they both sat on her old-fashioned couch and shifted around slightly until they were comfortable. The younger of the two, who had a small notebook out, asked her politely just what it was she wanted to report but she told them of course they must be thirsty because it certainly had been hot out lately and Lord knows how they work out in that heat all the time and then she bustled into the kitchen, got the lemonade and cookies on the tray and carefully carried it all back into the living room and set it down on the coffee table in front of the young officers and she saw that the older of the two looked at his partner and smiled and looked up at her and said Thank you very much and then as she watched approvingly he carefully poured two glasses full of lemonade and his younger partner said But there are only two glasses and she said, Really, it was for them and she didn't care for any . . . it was for them.

She sat down on the edge of one of her chairs with her back straight, head high, and waited for the young officers to both take a little drink from their goblets. Then the younger one picked up his notebook again and asked what it was she wanted to report so she told them about the lawn furniture she kept in the backyard and how some vandals had come and taken it all away and it was a shame really because she had owned it for years and she had lived there for years and while she spoke she saw that the older officer had taken a couple of the butter cookies and was trying to keep the crumbs from falling on the couch and that made her smile but anyway how she had lived there for years and how the neighborhood used to be so quiet and everyone got along just fine and it was so nice and she used to walk down the block to the church but not anymore it was just dreadful the way people were and the church had changed anyway and she really didn't know anyone who went there and she was saddened by the way people treated each other today, especially the younger ones and it was sad the way the neighborhood had changed and the way the vandals were so brazen anymore, going around stealing whatever they wanted and of course she felt so sorry for the young gentleman officers who had to go out and try to arrest those young hooligans and she just didn't know anymore.

She watched as the older officer carefully dusted the crumbs off his fingers onto the tray and then both officers stood and of course she stood too and the younger one asked if she could remember the color of the furniture and she told him it was yellow, really a pretty yellow, like bright yellow ribbon. The younger officer told her they would make a report, and they would watch her house from now on to make sure the vandals would stay away and she thought that was very nice and told him so. The older officer asked if he could look into the backyard, sort of visit the scene of the crime, and he stepped out onto the front porch. She said of course so he walked away and in a moment she heard him call to his partner who started to walk away but came back and offered her his arm as she stepped down from the porch, and she held onto his arm as they walked together around the side garden and into the backyard and she felt how strong the young officer was and how handsome he was and she just knew he had a lovely young lady waiting for him somewhere and it made her feel good and she remembered the handsome young men and how they came courting, but oh, that was so long ago and this was very exciting and what did the older officer want... had he found a clue?

When they reached the backyard she saw the older officer standing beside all the yellow lawn furniture and she clasped her hands to her breast in surprise. But how wonderful! How did he ever? The younger officer smiled and said maybe the vandals were scared off before they could get away with the goods and the older officer said maybe they had been bothered by a guilty conscience and it was a good thing she had called them so they could make sure the furniture was still there and they both smiled at her and my, it made her feel so safe to have strong young men like these officers watching her house.

Then they all walked back to the front porch, with her still holding onto the arm of the younger officer and she told them she was so happy they had come by and they helped her up onto the porch and the older one said Make sure you lock your door now and call us anytime and she said she would and God bless them and they turned and walked to their car. She stood on the porch and waved as they slowly drove away, and oh, remember how she used to stand on the porch and wave as he drove off, but no... no time for that now. There was so much cleaning up to do and she had to put everything away and my, they certainly liked those cookies and then she would fix a little dinner and listen to the radio for a while and my, that was exciting, and oh... what a busy day.

Looking back on my years on the force, and the times that I was dispatched to take reports or assist this woman, I imagine what it must have been like for her, watching the world hurrying by outside her small house. Once or twice, when the radio traffic wasn't busy and the jealous street wasn't calling my name, I was able to spend some time with her, listening while she told me of her life, her world, her daily fears and triumphs.

She was a beautiful woman.

Seventeen

I ALWAYS wished there were some way to capture the moment on the street, preserve it intact, with the sounds and smells and feels of the confrontation. It would have been so much easier for the judge, the jury, and the parents to understand why the brutal police officer had treated their young defendant/son so terribly.

The ones that shocked me the most were the beach maggots. Somehow there seemed to be a little extra filthy violence out on the "strip." The young drifters wound up there, the lost ones, the acidheads, PCP freaks, crack smokers, runaways, thieves, male whores... the whole lovely potpourri.

It is hard for people not in the business to understand, but a working cop very rarely confronts any citizen for just no reason. Citizens may look at the situation later and feel there was no reason for the officer to approach them, but they have no way of knowing what really motivated the officer. Cops just don't bother people for no reason.

Anyway, I walk up to the beach maggot. He is a white male in his late teens or early twenties. He has long dirty stringy hair to his shoulders, a lean muscular body, and dirty bare feet, or maybe heavy leather boots with a crushed-down look and big heels. He is wearing a pair of jeans that are ragged on the bottom from dragging on the street. He may have one or two homemade or jailhouse tattoos, or a pro job that says: *Born to lose*, or *Live hard, die young*. His walk is more of a swagger, his arms swinging at his sides, his hips rocking, and his lower back straight even though his shoulders are hunched. He has a bounce in his step, like he was a white kid trying hard to strut like a jive black dude. The expression on his face is one of mockery or disdain, or anger, or confusion, or a constantly changing kaleidoscope of them all. Inside the eyes are the clues that tell me he has recently ingested some chemical that has altered his mental-emotional state. He is stoned, and I don't mean mellow, life-is-fine-I-love-the-birds-and-the-sunshine-and-all-my-brothers-stoned either. The chemicals he is into trigger paranoia, aggressiveness, lack of reasoning, and violence.

He matches the description put out in briefing or on the radio for a burglary suspect that has been hitting the beach homes. Or he matches the description of a suspect who is selling PCP on the strip, or of a guy who is using a stolen credit card, or of a guy who robbed a tourist at knifepoint, or of one who was seen sleeping in a stolen car before the midnight shift guys towed it away. Or he matches the description of a suspect who managed to drag a fourteen-year-old girl into some bushes and get part of her clothes ripped off before he was chased away by a hotel maid. Charming.

So... for no reason at all I walk up to the maggot and say, "Excuse me, my man, hold it a minute, I'd like to talk to you."

"*What do you want, motherfucker? I don't hear you, man! Get away from me!*"

"Hey, guy... go easy, I just want to talk to you. Got some I.D.?"

"*Shit, man* ... I got I.D. ... but I don't have to show you *shit*, man. I didn't do *nuthin'!*"

"Nobody said you did anything, pal. Take it easy, okay?"

"I didn't do *nuthin'*, and you got *no right* to stop me!"

"Hey... it's just routine, that's all."

At this point I notice that the suspect is in a highly agitated, nervous state, and there is a noticeable bulge in one of his pockets. It could be a pocketknife. It could be an old hamburger.

It could be a soapdish full of marijuana, someone else's wallet, or a gun, a bag of Quaaludes, or a hairbrush.

"Well, look, guy... let's see some I.D. ... I just need to..."

"Get *away* from me, motherfucker! Don't *touch* me! Get your hand off my arm!"

"Look, get up against the wall, spread your legs, and relax. Step back... good... remember, the supreme of all courts says it's okay for me to do this... for your protection and mine."

"*Warrant!* You need a *warrant*, motherfucker! Get away from me ... hey, look, everybody! This fuckin' pig is hasslin' me ... hey, pig! Don't touch me, man, or you'll wish you'd never been born!*"

It is usually at this point that the maggot tells me either his father is an attorney and he will own me after he sues me for what I'm doing, or he tells me he is very bad and he's going to kick my ass.

A crowd begins to gather, and most of them don't like me anyway. It's time to control the situation. I grab the maggot, throw him against the wall while he screams, and pat him down. The bulge in his pocket is a packet of pills or a small bible.

Either way, I start to pull it out and the maggot pushes himself off the wall and swings his body around, arms flailing. Is he just trying to get away? Are his fists bunched because he's scared? Does he mean to hit me? Does he mean for his elbow to crash into the side of my head?

As he turns I knee him hard in the groin, then I give him a short, close, vicious chop in the throat. He starts to go down, and I want to keep hitting him. I want to smash my fist into his filthy mouth, I want to see his blood on my hands. I want to kick him and stomp him and put him away.

But I don't.

Once he goes down onto the sidewalk he covers his head with his hands and cowers there, screaming,

"*Help! Help!* The fuckin' pigs is beatin' me! I'm being beaten *for no reason!* My lip is cut! Oooh, *motherfucker*... you're going to pay for this! *Oooohhh!*"

I cuff him, stand him on his feet, and shuffle him off to my unit. On the way he must still perform for the crowd, screaming and twisting around... a real tough guy now that he's in the protective womb of the handcuffs... begging for witnesses and help. What an asshole.

Into the car. Into the station. Into booking.

Later that day I go to the supply room to trade in my uniform pants with the knee torn out and to get a new hat to replace the one stolen from the sidewalk while I struggled with the maggot. My cut fingers or scraped elbow don't bleed much, but they bother me when I wear long-sleeved shirts for a couple of days.

Guess who comes to court a couple of months later looking like wholesome Middle America himself? He is usually with at least one parent (the mother... who looks patiently defensive of her son, and who shoots me withering glances of disapproval while shaking her head) and a pin-striped attorney who has already taken fifteen hundred dollars from mom and will get more with his promises of a lucrative lawsuit. The young man is charged with misdemeanors: possession of grass, resisting arrest, battery on a cop...some such thing.

I wish I could tell the judge and the jury and his mom about his dirty feet and his filthy loud mouth. I wish I could tell them about the spacey look in his eyes, about the way he smelled, about the vibrating pulsing charging antagonism that emanated from him. The way his skin felt, the way his stomach muscles tightened before he hit me. The word games he used with the crowd. I wish I could paint for them an accurate picture of the maggot I met on the beach the day of the arrest.

But I can't.

The rules of the game and the tactics of the defense attorney won't let me. I can only recite bare, skeletal facts, and these I must fight for every inch of the way. The trim, clean young man sitting there in the business suit hardly fits the person I try to tell the courtroom about.

Sometimes when it is over I am admonished by the judge, ridiculed professionally by the defense attorney, and sued by the mom. Sometimes the city ends up paying mom and her lawyer to avoid a costly fight in civil court, even if it means letting my principles fall neglected into the dirt. Sometimes I get a letter of reprimand in my file, or a day off without pay for "excessive use of force."

Sometimes I could give a damn.

A maggot is a maggot is a maggot.

Eighteen

"HEY, HONEY... I'm home. Sorry I'm late, had a bunch of paper-work to do. We still going out tonight?"

Silence.

"Hey... you okay? How was school today, learn some good stuff?"

"Have you seen the newspaper? The story about what happened yesterday? The *front-page* story?"

"Yeah... crazy paper went wild with it, didn't they? It's..."

"It's a front-page story about how you and your partner beat up this poor kid after he had an accident in his car! Of *course* they went wild! Witnesses said the kid was just walking away ... you were seen beating him after he was handcuffed, with your radio! *Jesus.*"

"Don't drag Him into this..."

"Oh, it's something we can joke about, right? Do you know my mother has already called me... she's so upset? She's afraid the neighbors are going to blackball me from the laundry room or something."

"C'mon, honey... the papers don't have it..."

"And my *friends!* You don't think they know I'm married to a cop? They already ask me how I do it, and after this..."

"After this, *what?* Honey, it's just a newspaper story... sure, it's front-page stuff now because they've got it all bent out of shape! Six weeks from now, after the in-department review board clears me and the state attorney's office clears me, the story will cover maybe two lines back on the last damn page. Don't worry about it."

"Oh, you're going to get away with this one? What if you get time off without pay? How much is this going to cost us?"

"Goddamn it! Did the paper mention that the kid crashed a stolen car into a house? Did they mention that he was coked out of his skull, that he has a record for auto theft and battery on a cop? If I break my police radio I have to *pay* for it! You think I'm gonna chance that on some scroatbag's head when I can do a better job with my hands?"

Pause.

"Listen, honey... the paper doesn't have the whole story, and they don't *want* the whole story. They just want to sell papers."

"Your name... and *my* name, now... is still spread all over the front page. In that story you sound like every other overly aggressive cop out there, like a monster. Why can't you just take it easy?"

"You took my name willingly! Do you want to change it back?"

Silence. Locking stares.

"Crap. Honey... this stuff just happens. Look, we're supposed to go out tonight, right? We're going to see your friends, a get-together of the school crowd. Let's get ready, relax, and go to the party. We'll have a good time, and I promise not to start any discussions about the Supreme Court. C'mon, get those perfect buns into something tight, brush out that lovely hair, and we'll go."

"I don't know if I feel like..."

"What? I thought you *wanted* to go to this one... all your educated and liberated girlfriends, and even that favorite 'brilliant' professor of yours."

Silence.

"Would you rather I stayed home and you went to the party alone, without your monster husband and his tarnished name?"

She went without me, and in retrospect I see that my name was firmly printed on her driver's license, but it was fading from her heart.

Nineteen

It was a dark and stormy night.

No, seriously, it really was. No moon, heavily overcast, gusty wind, and lots of drizzly rain.

I'm working the beach area and I get an "unknown trouble" call at this address over in the Harbor Beach area. This is an expensive residential neighborhood made up of islands connected to each other by small bridges. Every house in the area is big, plush, and on the water. This is where the society page lives, the backbone of the financial community. Funny money, new money, dope money, old money, real money . . . it's all here.

So I get this call and I drive through the drizzle looking for the address and when I pull up in front of the house I see that all of the lights are off. I get out of my car and walk across the gravel drive and see a Cadillac in the carport, and as I shine the beam of my flashlight around I see that the carport door leading into the house is slightly ajar. I walk up to the door and listen for a moment but I don't hear anything so I open the door and look in. The door leads to a small hallway that leads to the kitchen. Standing at the sink, in the darkness, is a man. He is facing the sink, looking out the small window there, and he is wearing a robe. I don't want to shine my light in his face but I flash it around the kitchen to get his attention but he doesn't move. He just stands there with his feet slightly spread and his hands on the sink top. I can see he is wearing slippers and there is a small dog by his feet. The dog doesn't bark, but perks up his ears, cocks his head, and looks at me. As far as I can tell, the rest of the house is dark. I clear my throat, hoping to attract the man's attention, but he still acts like he does not know I'm there. I take a better look at him and I can see he is old, his hair is white and the skin of his neck is wrinkled into folds. He is staring out the window and I'm beginning to get nervous because I can't figure out what is going on. I say, "Pssst" to the man and he still doesn't react, so I figure he's scared. He's afraid to say anything because there's someone in the house. It's a damn in-progress situation of some kind.

I don't want to take a chance on letting the situation slide by waiting for a backup, and I know the dispatcher is sending one anyway because of the unknown nature of the call. So I step into the hallway, draw my gun, and walk quickly past the old man and the dog toward the living room. As I go by them I say quietly, "Stay here," but he doesn't answer and the dog just watches me so I keep moving.

Once in the living room I can see that there has been a party of some kind. The place is a mess, with empty glasses and bottles lying all over the place, ashtrays all filled, and food trays here and there. I shine my light around the room quickly and then move toward the bedrooms, knowing if there is a burglar in the house that's where he'll be. By the time I carefully but quickly check all three bedrooms I'm becoming more mystified. I find no one and there is no sign of ransacking. I figure it's time to go back and ask the old man what the hell is going on so I walk back through the darkened house to the kitchen.

When I get there I see that the old man hasn't moved an inch, he's still standing there hanging on to the sink for dear life. I walk up beside him and shine the light in his face and say, "Okay, sir...what's the problem here?" He doesn't even blink an eye and I'm getting a sinking feeling and I know I'm not going to like it but I reach out slowly and touch his left hand and then I know.

There's something about a dead body that is just unmistakable to the touch. When I touched his cold hard hand I knew ...there was no doubt about it.

He was standing dead at the sink.

Now the small dog gets up on its legs and starts to growl at me, apparently because I've discovered his master's secret. I can feel the hair on the back of my neck stand up and I back away carefully from both of them. I give them all the room I can in the small kitchen, and head for the door. I hurry through the carport and across the gravel drive to my car, looking over my shoulder the whole time.

From the street I can see the shadow of the old man in the kitchen, with the dog settling down by his feet. As I watch a stillness comes over the house, and the darkness seems to deepen and I stand huddled in the rain, waiting for the old man to wave at me and call out that he's okay, but he doesn't, and as an eerie silence settles on the area, I look around in the darkness and wish I were somewhere else. Anywhere else.

But I'm not, I'm here.

Me, the dog, and the dead man.

Twenty

THE STRIP on New Year's Eve.

Can you imagine? The very same part of the beach I used to come to as a kid with my parents. We would get cherry Cokes at the drugstore fountain and waffle ice-cream sandwiches down the street near the old Casino Pool.

It was clean then, sunny and nice. The people were different, we were all different. The beach was a nice place for the family to go on a weekend to be together and enjoy what Fort Lauderdale was supposed to be all about.

The strip on New Year's Eve is nothing like that. I'm leaning against the wall, in uniform, watching the people drift by.

Drunk, dirty, drugged, nasty, filthy, spaced-out, leering laughing giggling spitting cursing crying shrieking stumbling falling pushing, fighting gaggles of street types making their abrasive way from one end of the strip to the other. Happy New Year . . . we're all assholes and we're going nowhere.

I don't want to be there, obviously.

Anyway, there I am, trying to stay out of the way and just make it through the night. I'm leaning against the wall at the entrance to a video-game arcade when it happens.

Clinging hands clutch at my ears, wet lips press against mine, and a slick rubbery probing darting searching tongue invades my mouth and penetrates almost into my throat. I push away with my hands and jerk my head back hard. The tongue and lips and hands fall away.

Shocked, I look down at my attacker.

There, standing in front of me, is an honest-to-God *primo* example of a female street maggot (maggotess?). She is not very tall, and not very old, and not very clean at all. She has long straight brown hair that is greasy and clings to her bare shoulders. She wears a silver metallic-looking tube top with no bra, and it is easy to see that when she takes it off her still young but oh-so-old breasts will sag against her pudgy belly. She has stuffed her already heavy thighs into dirty jeans and her feet are black, black with street dirt and filth. She has painted a face for herself with glitter eye makeup and rouge, and she has thickened her pouty lips with a heavy layer of greenish lipstick. Her skin is oily and sweaty and pocked with acne, even the skin of her shoulders.

She smells bad.

She needs badly to shave under her arms and brush her teeth. She needs badly to wash her hair. She needs badly to bathe repeatedly three times a day until further notice. She needs badly to stop drinking and taking Quaaludes at the same time. She needs badly to get out of the apartment she is crashing in with two other girls and who knows how many guys from the street. She needs badly to go home to the small town in Michigan or Iowa or Ohio or New York or wherever. She needs to call her parents and have them come and get her yesterday.

She needs to be hosed down, bagged, and shipped home C.O.D.

She stands there looking up at me with a leer on her grotesque-pathetic face and her hands on her hips. She sways slightly on her spread legs, giggles, and blurts out, "Happy Fucking New Year Piggly-Wiggly!" Then she sticks out her tongue, winks at me lewdly, and pouts, "If you think you can handle it, little police-man, I'll show you *another* place where I'm pink on the inside!" Then she turns away, looks over her shoulder at me, gives her greasy hair a toss, and walks off, blending in with the crowd and disappearing quickly.

I stand there wiping her spit off my face, wondering where I'm going to find a quart of penicillin mixed with paint thinner to gargle with.

Twenty-One

I ALWAYS thought it was a good thing Leo was a cop. Because if he wasn't a cop he would have been a Bulgarian border guard, or one of those OPEC guys with the sheet for a suit, driving around in a gold Mercedes with a couple of hundred thousand dollars on his fingers. I mean, Leo was *swarthy*. Gypsy, with flashing eyes, a huge hook nose, a blacker-than-black mustache and curly hair. The guys called him Camel Jockey, and he looked it. But he did have this thing: he *did* come up with the felony grabs. He was always making some big arrest, you know, stolen car or hot burglar. When asked about it he'd just grin and say, "It's all in the wrist."

So it's Saturday night in the middle of the summer and I'm for some reason working blacktown with Leo and we're cruising Sistrunk Boulevard real slow lookin' at the show . . . all the hookers and pimps and drunks and junkies and crackheads and badasses and the whole thing, you know. It's real hot and sultry and it's for sure we're gonna see a couple of cuttings and at least one shooting before the night's over and we pull up to the curb near one of those little roadside barbecue stands that they have with the grill made out of half a fifty-five-gallon drum and the old Aunt Jemima-type lady standin' in the blue smoke cookin' up those ribs. You've seen it.

We pull up there because Leo has gone about a half hour with no food and it's getting to him so here we are and we're standing there and Leo's doing a number on about a half pound of ribs when we hear this little voice say, "Hey Mister po-lice. Mister po-lice. I can't find my momma."

We look down and here's this little niglet standing there in his bare feet, wearing nothing but an old pair of gym shorts that are too big and raggedy at the bottom. His fuzzy head is half white with dirt and you could see where he'd been cryin' because the tears had run lines across the layer of fine dirt on his face. His lower lip was stuck out about a half mile as he said, "Please Mister po-lice. Help me find my momma."

Crap. Musta been all of six years old. Out on nasty-ass Sistrunk almost midnight and I figure for sure ol' Aunt Jemima here knows where his momma is but she just looks away. So now I figure, here it is Saturday night and there's gonna be some good shit goin' down and we gotta screw around with this kid. Before I can really begin to stew about it Leo looks down at the kid and says, "Well, where do you think your momma went, little guy?"

The kid looks up at Leo like Leo was Martin Luther King or somebody and says, "She's out drinkin', Mister po-lice. But I don't know where." He looks like he wants to cry but I can see he's holding it back and you just know he's gonna be a tough sonofabitch when he grows up but right now here we are and it's Saturday night in the summer on Sistrunk and shit.

Leo wipes the barbecue sauce off his hands and puts his left down for the kid and says, "C'mon, little man, let's go find momma." The kid wraps one hand around Leo's big fat index finger and asks, "What we gonna do?" and Leo just says, "Follow me," and off they go, down the sidewalk, hand in finger. As they walk away Leo looks over at me and winks and I know he wants me to follow along so I lock up the unit and come behind, watching the pink soles of the kid's feet as he hikes along beside Leo, occasionally hitching up his old blue shorts.

Let me tell you, we had some really classy places right there in that area. I mean the Eight Ball Pool Emporium and Big Joe's and The Blackjack and Whitey's and the Klub Kool, you know, and all those places are just somethin' else but here we go...me, Leo, and the kid, who is still hanging on to Leo's finger for dear life. I'll tell ya, I felt like hangin' onto his finger too when we walked into a couple of those places.

It's like this. We walk in and stand there for a minute to get our eyes adjusted to the dim light. There's a lot of scurryin' around because as soon as we walk in the crap games break up and all kinda dudes are makin' it for the bathroom where they can either flush their stash or pass it out the back window to the alley. It gets kinda quiet at first with all of em' trying to see what the police are gonna do. Is this a roust or what, man? Then, when they see the kid stickin' to Leo's finger they kinda talk among themselves, but nobody laughs. I'm stayin' tight because I just can't relax, you know, but Leo's walking around like he owns the place, showing the kid the sights. Then he goes over to the bar and grabs the barkeep and gets his face real close and asks if anybody is talking about missing their kid but all we get is a shake of the head so Leo walks to the middle of the room (people kinda slidin' outta the way...you know how they do) and lifts the kid up and stands him on a table and says to him, "Look around, little guy, and tell me if you see your momma," and the kid looks around, but hell, he's scared and he don't see her anyway and it's Saturday night and it's hot and bull*shit*.

So here we go back out onto the sidewalk and at least it's slightly cooler and there's a breeze and we go walking toward the next joint, the kid still clinging desperately to Leo's finger and Leo's asking him if he ever heard of Segovia and the kid is sayin', "How come you jingle when you walk?" and we're just having a hell of a time.

Finally we come out of the Melody Dance Hall with the kid and I'm getting kinda tired of this whole gig but Leo looks like he's just gettin' started when the kid breaks down and starts cryin' a little, grabbing the ragged sides of his shorts and snuf-flin' and blowin' all over the place and I'm thinkin', shit, and Leo's patting the kid on the head and saying, "Just hang in there, kid, we'll find her," and the kid looks up at Leo like he believes him and I wish I could believe him when we hear a screech and the next thing we know there's this orange-haired woman in tight purple pants hitting Leo on his curly head and yellin', "Help! Help! The honky po-lice done stealin' my moth-erfuckin' baby boy!" and stuff like that and I'm trying to get around to her and people are beginning to come out onto the sidewalk and Leo's coverin' his head and the kid's wrapped around one of Leo's legs and holy shit, you've never seen such a thing in your life. Finally Leo holds the kid up in front of him, like you would hold up garlic to keep a vampire away, and says, "Hold it a moment, miss . . ." and the orange-haired lady stops screaming and grabs the kid and turns on her heel and stalks off, down the sidewalk toward a big two-and-a-quarter Electra parked against the curb with some dude behind the wheel wearing a white suit and a big wide-brimmed bright red hat. Shit.

So I look at Leo and he looks at me and we both stand there waving bye-bye to the kid who is lookin' back over his momma's shoulder and wriggling his little fingers at us. He's smilin' and Leo's smilin' and hell, it's Saturday night and it's hot and here we are on ol' Sistrunk about five hundred miles from the friggin' car and Leo says, "Cute little guy, huh, Cherokee?"

Twenty-Two

I WAS working day shift in the northwest section of town and had a new guy named Jim riding with me. It had been a routine day, and we only had a couple of hours to go when the dispatcher advised us of a "suspicious incident." A citizen had reported seeing two white males climbing around the second story of an office building. It was the weekend and all the offices in that building were closed. We headed that way.

As we pulled up into the back lot we saw that one of the upstairs windows was broken open. The building was split-level at that point, so you could stand on the roof of the first floor and climb into the window, gaining access to all the offices on the second floor. We advised the dispatcher we would check it out, and had little difficulty in finding a way to climb up to the roof and then over to the window.

As we moved across the gravel on the roof we could hear pounding noises coming from inside the offices, and as we moved up against the window, one on either side, we came face to face with a young white guy with a lot of curly red hair and freckles. He was wearing jeans, with no shoes or shirt, and he was munching on an apple. I pushed my service revolver through the window, stuck it in the guy's face, and yelled, "Freeze, asshole!" The guy looked at me, at the gun, took a bite of the apple, turned, and walked away from us, down the hallway toward the offices.

Jim and I looked at each other and climbed in after him. We

hurried down the hallway and found that all the office doors had been kicked in. The interiors of the offices were all in shambles, everything thrown around, desks turned over, pictures ripped from the walls, and file cabinets gutted, papers strewn everywhere. Stacked neatly by the doorways of the offices were piles of typewriters, adding machines, tape recorders, and other valuables. We quickly checked all of the offices looking for the red-haired guy, and found him waiting for us in the last one.

Jim stepped in first and said, "Hold it right there..." and the guy's eyes widened, he let out a scream, and he went berserk. He jumped, he kicked, he tore our shirts. He punched and bit and gouged. He grunted and snarled and laughed and screamed obscenities. We tried all the official restraining holds, and his naked sweaty arms kept squirming loose and hurting us, so we finally resorted to the old tried-and-true method of simply beating the shit out of him. Then we handcuffed him and stood up panting. I stayed with him while Jim checked the rest of the building. He finally found the second guy, small and dark-haired and quiet, crunched up underneath a sink in a little wooden cabinet. Jim cuffed him with no trouble and dragged him out through the window and had him sit on the roof while I brought the red-haired guy down the hallway.

I left him standing beside Jim while I went back to make an examination of the offices to determine who belonged to what, who to call, all that. I was advising the dispatcher of what we had when I heard a struggle and looked down the hallway to see the red-haired guy violently kicking and head-butting Jim, who was trying to keep away from the blows and still contain the guy. Knowing the second one was still out on the roof, and seeing Jim take a couple of hits, I started running as hard as I could toward the struggle.

By this time I had had it with the red-haired asshole. It would be fair to say I was pissed off.

I waited until I was about six feet from the guy, at a dead run, and I jumped into the air and brought my legs up and let my street shoes impact the guy's face and chest. He was slammed into the wall and then crushed down onto the floor with me on top of him.

He stopped struggling.

Jim, panting, looked down at the guy, looked at me, and grinned.

We dragged the red-haired guy onto the roof alongside the quiet dark-haired one and waited for some help to get them down. It was late in the day, and the afternoon sun was warm. We stood there, breathing easily, looking down at our two burglars. The small dark one just sat there, his mouth slack, his eyes far away. The red-haired guy lay on his side and belly, his hands cuffed behind him. His eyes were open wide, and he writhed around and kicked his feet and hunched his shoulders. He hissed and gurgled and grunted and growled and giggled and gagged. He was bloody and sweaty and dirty and he smelled like vomit and urine and sweat.

Jim and I stood there waiting, relaxed, while the red-haired burglar lay at our feet eating mouthfuls of gravel on the roof.

Twenty-Three

STUPID BASTARD.

That's what I thought as I pushed against the men's room door at the gas station. My partner and I had been dispatched there in reference to a "suspicious incident"; the station manager had called about someone being in the bathroom and not letting anyone use it. The manager told us of all the trouble he had been having lately with the kids from the adjoining neighborhood using his bathroom at night as a place to hide and get high, and trashing the place.

The service station was on Sunrise Boulevard, one of the main streets of the city, and was bordered on the south side by a large black residential section. It was near a park with ballfields and a swimming pool, in an area that stayed busy most of the night. The station had been open all night for a while, but the robberies got so bad it wasn't worth it anymore. I had answered calls there before about gasoline ripoffs and junkies loitering. The manager was a middle-aged black man with a large belly and an easy grin. He usually had a dirty rag in his hand and walked around with an air of immense patience. He only called the police when he absolutely had to. This was one of those times.

He told us he had found several young black guys at various times of the week sleeping in the bathroom when he opened in the morning. The bathroom was not locked anymore since he had to keep replacing the lock every time it was. He told us he would usually stand there, pounding on the metal door until they dragged themselves up off the floor, and then he would yell at them and chase them away. He told us that on this morning he found the door partly open, and when he tried to move it the rest of the way, it stuck. He pounded on it and yelled but whoever was in there wouldn't come out. He could just see a pair of sneakers on the floor, and part of a leg, so he knew someone was in there. Whoever it was, however, had ignored him and now he was fed up and tired of trying to be decent with these damn kids around here anyway and why couldn't the police do something about it? Why couldn't the police watch his station at night so he wouldn't find this kind of problem in the morning? Then he walked away, leaving us with the stupid bastard in the bathroom.

My partner and I pounded on the door and shouted and yelled and tried to push the door open but the guy inside wouldn't budge. He ignored us. Every time I pushed on the door it would give a little, but then it would slide closed again. Sonofabitch. I took my Mace out of my belt, placed it against the crack in the door, and gave it a little squirt. That should have made him squirm around some. Nothing. I stood on my toes and peered through the crack. I could see, barely, what looked like a black guy lying on his side on the floor of the bathroom. I could only see part of the legs, the upper part of his body was against the door.

I turned to my partner and said, "Uh-oh."

While my partner pushed as hard as he could against the door I turned sideways and scraped through into the bathroom. My man was wearing an old sweatshirt with the sleeves pushed up past his elbows, a pair of shorts, and the sneakers. He had a rubber tube wrapped around his arm and clenched in his teeth. A hypodermic needle stuck out of his arm. The spoon and cooker were in the sink.

He was very dead. Stiff dead. Teak dead. Dead with intent to block the door. Dead with his feet against one wall and his head and shoulders crammed against the door, forcing it closed.

Seventeen years old.

He was a seventeen-year-old junkie lying in the filth of the gas station bathroom, blocking the door closed with his head.

I looked down into the sweaty face with the half-open eyes, the flared nostrils, the lips pulled back, and the teeth clenched around that rubber tube.

Stupid bastard.

Twenty-Four

PARANOID POLICE officer.

That's what I was told. I was a paranoid cop because I was dead set against giving out my home address.

Given my normal dealings with the world, there was no way I could be forced to tell anyone where I lived. It was my private place, and I didn't want to have to tell anyone where it was.

An angry cop is not a thinking cop. A cop on the defensive is not a thinking cop either, he just might miss something that is important. It was easy for an attorney to get me angry, or to put me on the defensive. All he had to do was ask me for my home address during any questioning. This usually occurred during deposition, before the trial, when the defense attorney is trying to learn what the cop knows and how well he can present it in court. Even though it had nothing to do with the arrest or evidence at all, the attorney would ask for my home address near the beginning of the questioning. I would usually rattle off "Thirteen hundred West Broward Boulevard," and if the attorney wasn't sharp I would get away with it. If he knew that was the address of the police station he would ask me again, and advise me he could get the question "certified" if I resisted. This meant he could take the question before a judge, who would usually find that the attorney was within his rights and the workings of the case to have that information, and order me to answer it or be in contempt. All judges have at one time been attorneys.

I knew all this and would eventually have to give the attorney my home address, and I would already be steamed.

Why? What was the big deal? Why should I get upset at having to give an attorney who represents someone I've arrested my home address?

I'll give you *one* incident. Just one in ten years.

It wasn't a big arrest. I had stopped this guy named Brown in the south end, and other than an expired driver's license he had no I.D. or papers for the car he was driving. I had watched him cruise around a small business district slowly for a while. It was late, the businesses were closed, and I wanted to check him out.

He had a gun under the seat, and a small bag of grass in his pocket. No big deal, but he had to go to jail, and I had to tow his car.

We were still sitting, waiting for the wrecker, him in the backseat of my unit, when he started. He was pissed. This was a humbug, and it was all happening because he was black. I was a honky motherfucker, and was just rousting him because he was a black man, and if I didn't have a gun and badge he would kick my ass, and would anyway if he ever got the chance.

I sat there listening to him, filling out the primary arrest forms and nodding my head in agreement every once in a while. I had heard it all before, too many times. No big deal.

I listened to him tell me what he was going to do to me all the way to the jail. I was tired, and he wasn't telling me anything new. I was a cop, he really didn't see me, and it was nothing personal. He could be upset with me if he wanted. He could threaten to hurt me, because it wasn't me he was talking to, it was a cop. A white cop. I could live with that.

So we got to the jail and I took him out of the car and got into the old jail elevator with him. He stood on one side of the metal grille, and I stood on the other while we waited for someone upstairs to push the button for our slow ascent to the booking area.

By this time Brown had really worked himself into a lather. He was literally foaming and sweating and twitching around.

He got his face close to the grill and hissed, "Hey, honky motherfucker. I'll bet you got a little wife with long blonde hair at
home . . . don't you?"

I looked at him. Inside I was startled. I *did* have a blonde
wife at home.

"Well listen here, paddy po-lice. One of these days I'm gonna
come round your house, hear me? You won't be there, little
boy, but that sweet woman of yours will be, huh? I'll be goin'
in there boy, and I'll fuck your ol' lady so hard she'll be cryin',
my man . . . she'll be cryin' for more of what I got for her! And
when I get done wid her, man, I'll cut her throat out and let
her bleed to death all over your little pretend home . . ."

His words knocked me back against the far wall of the elevator. I pictured what he said in my mind, and it frightened
and repelled me. I stared at him and saw him slinking around
my yard, stalking through my living room, forcing his way into
my bedroom, doing what he said.

I stared at him and went cold.

He stood there on the other side of the grille, grinning.

I had the grille partly open and was on my way after him
when the elevator door opened and the jail lieutenant stepped
in to help me with my prisoner. Brown stood there grinning
and the lieutenant grabbed him by the arm and walked him
out to the booking desk. Brown stepped lightly across the floor,
looked over his shoulder at me, and got himself safely booked.

Listen, I have to give you just one *more* that happened . . . sort
of round it out for you.

I spent some time as an undercover narcotics officer. I worked
against street dealers and drug traffickers while in the Marine
Patrol Unit, and was involved in international smuggling cases
while on loan to a special countywide task force. Working undercover, especially against people who play for keeps, means
being vulnerable. You wear an undercover persona, a false skin,
and you work hard to distance yourself from your real identity
and your real life. As an undercover cop I would say things and

do things and go places and relate in various ways to people and activities that would never be a part of the person that was me at home.

During the final wrap-up of a long and complex international case that saw many indictments and much property and drugs and money seized, depositions and other legal formalities were taking place. I was in a room at the courthouse with a prosecutor, a defense attorney, a court reporter, and the defendant, who was a local businessman-turned-smuggler. This guy was one of the top men in the structure we had just taken down, he faced many years in the graybar hotel, and he wanted to play hardball.

A couple of days before the deposition I got a telephone call at home. The caller was a business acquaintance of the defendant, also involved in local business, legitimate as far as I knew. My mother owned her own business and was a CPA. The caller advised me he was calling on behalf of the defendant and several others who just wanted me to know they knew who I was, knew I was a local boy, and knew my mother and where her business was. Then he hung up.

During the deposition I played it by the book, giving direct answers and biding my time. The defendant sat back with his lawyer, staring at me and looking quite confident. When the proceedings were winding down I looked at the prosecutor and stated that I wanted to make a statement for the record. He was noncommittal, frowning and shrugging his shoulders. The defendant looked confused, and his defense attorney nodded, secretly pleased. He knew the more a cop said on the record, the more chance there was to trip him up later.

When I had their attention I told them of the phone call to my home. I told them the caller had identified the defendant as one he spoke for. By this time the defendant was already protesting, but his lawyer quieted him down. I told them, for the record, that my mother had received a call shortly after I had, and that the caller just wanted her to know that my identity was known, as was hers. Both attorneys looked uncomfortable with things by this point, and the defendant's face began to redden.

Now as I spoke I began throwing things at the defendant's face to make sure he paid attention to my words. Just paper clips at first, and then the odd pencil and pen. What I told him for the record was simple. If, at any time during the trial or follow-up legal proceedings, or at *any* time in the future, my mother heard *one word* about the case from anyone but me, or if *I* heard anyone say one word to me or anyone else about my mother or any member of my family about the case, then there would be no case.

The prosecutor was beginning to pale, and the defense attorney's look of glee was quickly changing to one of dismay. The defendant sat there dumbfounded, acutely concerned, and peppered with my words and the missiles I hurled.

There would be no case, I went on, because there would be no defendant. He would be dead. I would kill him. There could be no mistake.

The room went dead silent. I looked him in the eye and could see the recognition and the fear, and I said, "Think about it."

After I left the courthouse I spent several days making sure that same message got out onto the street, to the right ears, including the friendly businessman who had made the calls. He took it badly, soiling his trousers after the full impact of what I had to say hit him.

I fully expected administrative and legal hassles for my actions, but none came. I never heard another word about it, and never went to trial on that defendant. He made a deal with the prosecutor's office, pleaded guilty, and went bye-bye for a while.

Maybe, after all the game playing he and his hardball partners had done, all the theater, maybe he had seen something in me that gave him pause.

I used to pray that if somehow, some way, some filth from my job spilled over and onto my lawn and into my home I would be there when it happened. I used to pray that if it was going to happen to let me get home early that day, to please get me home in time.

I used to promise myself and the Lord that if it ever happened I would not need my service revolver or any other store-bought weapon.

I would take care of the problem immediately and forever with my bare hands.

Twenty-Five

"*HEEELLLP MEEE... oh, heeelllp meeeeee....!*"

We stood there by the Florida East Coast Railroad trestle in the quiet of the night and tried to pinpoint where the moaning, pleading voice came from.

"*Heeelllp meeeeee...!*"

It was late and still, and the sound of the voice echoed and bounded all around. It was eerie.

My partner and I had been sent to the area on another "suspicious incident" report; someone was calling for help. Well, that was certainly true, now if we could just find the guy we could do something about it.

Finally I grabbed my partner's arm and pointed up. The railroad trestle was in the open position, the *up* position, so traffic on the river, if there was any at this hour, could go by. The trestle would automatically lower when a north or south-bound train was a preset distance away. My partner and I stood there staring up into the night sky. Faintly outlined against the stars was the upside-down figure of a man hanging by one leg from the very tip-top of the trestle, his arms spread wide, and his voice calling, "*Heelllp meee... !*"

The Flying Wino had been making his contented way south along the railroad tracks and had come to the river. He had looked carefully along the river in both directions, clutched his soul-sustaining bottle to his chest, and started to cross the railroad bridge to the other side. He was more than halfway across when he felt the very ground rising beneath him. He tried to hurry but found himself walking higher and higher up an ever-increasing hill. Finally he found himself climbing almost straight up, but he kept going anyway, determined to reach the top to see what was going on. Then it was too steep. It was like tearing out a piece of his heart, but he had to let his bottle go as he grabbed and lunged and took one last step over the top, only to find nothing there but moist air, and the black water of the river one hundred feet below him. He screamed and fell headlong, but as he fell one foot slipped down between the tracks and and the beams and wedged there. He felt a sharp pain in his ankle, and found himself dangling head-down in the night, swaying out over the river and calling plaintively to whoever might hear him.

And a train was coming.

My partner and I climbed up onto the tracks and stood beside the upraised trestle. No way. Even if we managed to climb up there it would be a total bitch to get him untangled and carry him down with us. We got on the radio to the dispatcher and asked her to contact the railroad, advise them of our problem, and get the train stopped. Then we called up to the Flying Wino to hang on, help was coming. He just called back, "*Heeelllp meee... !*"

And the train was still coming.

We jumped into our unit and went racing through town and over the Andrews Avenue Bridge to get to the south side of the river.

That was where the tip of the trestle would rest when in the lowered position. We skidded to a stop and jumped out and heard the sound of the gears and the motors on the other side of the trestle. It was going to come down.

And... the train was *still* coming.

We got back to the dispatcher to ask why the train hadn't been stopped and why the trestle was closing. She replied that the train had to be contacted by radio from Jacksonville and our communications guys were trying to do that now. She didn't know why the trestle was closing but we guessed it was on a timer of some sort. If it closed on the Flying Wino, he was going to look like one hundred pounds of meatloaf marinated in a gallon of cheap port wine and stuffed into a five-pound bag.

We stood there craning our necks as the Flying Wino made his uncontrolled descent. He waved his arms and spun around and jackknifed his body up and down and I'm sure if there had been a scout for Barnum and Bailey in the area he would have gotten a job as understudy with the world-renowned Flying Zucchini Brothers.

And yes, incredibly, the train was still making its inexorable way toward this pathetic yet somehow stirring bid for survival.

My partner and I waited there with our arms outstretched. We figured we had a couple of seconds as the trestle reached our level to grab the Flying Wino and jerk him out of his predicament before the trestle and the base of the tracks came together with said Flying Wino as a gasket. We asked the dispatcher if she could send one of the northwest units to park on one of the crossings with his lights flashing to force the train to stop. We encouraged her to reach Jacksonville yesterday to find out how to stop the trestle from lowering itself onto our daring young man. Then we waited.

"*Heeelllp meee... !*" wailed the Flying Wino as he was lowered closer and closer to us. He could see what was happening now and was reaching out to us, hoping we'd have time to pull him out. We stood balanced on the tracks with our toes, stretching up and leaning out over the river. We were trying to get him and be careful at the same time. It certainly wouldn't do for one of us to slip and fall to the base of the tracks either. Not at all.

We barely got our hands on him and felt him clutching at us when we realized how fast the trestle was descending. It was really moving and we would have just seconds to do the job and if he was wedged in there it was going to be tough and the damn train was still coming and why the hell hadn't I called in sick on that night anyway...

And the trestle gave a jerk and stopped.

Someone somewhere had managed to pull a lever or hit a button and the trestle's wino-compacting descent was arrested, as he would be shortly when I got my sweaty little hands on him. A couple of young guys who felt athletic and didn't mind getting dirty came along and helped us pull the Flying Wino from his perch. Then they left and we were left with the aero-inebriate, who had a broken ankle but was thrilled to be in the firm custody of the police.

And the train continued its majestic way southbound, un-ruffled by the whole affair. We took the Flying Wino to the emergency room to have his ankle set, and then we took him in and booked him for Disorderly Intoxication (aerial display without a permit, interrupting flow of nighthawks in search of food, littering a famous waterway, hurling a wine bottle into the confines of the city from a height exceeding fifty feet, and disturbing police officers in pursuit of peace and quiet). He was pleased.

He told us later, "You know, the seats aren't too great, but that view is really something."

Twenty-Six

"OH BOY... here we go again..."

"What? What's the problem, honey?"

"You. Every time we get in the car you have to reach over across me and lock my door. It's becoming one of those little things that make me crazy."

"Well, you forget to lock your door even though I'm always reminding you, so I just do it, that's all."

"Fine, my door is locked. What do you think is going to happen, some bad person is going to run along beside us at thirty miles an hour, open the door, reach in and take my purse while he fondles my breasts?"

"He'd *have* to run that fast to get a chance to fondle your breasts..."

"Oh... cheap shot."

"Well, shit. You know that's not what it is. Suppose we stop at a red light? People get their purses ripped off all the time at red lights, it only takes a second. Besides, I'm just trying to get you in the habit of doing it, of thinking security out here."

"Out here? In the world? Out here in the bad world where we all have to go around freaked out all the time because at any moment we might be somehow victimized?"

"Goddammit..."

"You don't just lock the car doors, either. You lock the house. Christ, you lock the house when we're in it. You lock the house when we go down the street to the laundry! It's making me crazy..."

"Honey, it's just that you don't see—"

"I see someone with a siege mentality, always peering at the world through a keyhole. Are you locking them out or yourself in?"

Twenty-Seven

"EXCUSE ME, bailiff. Can you tell me if the Union Seventy-Six robbery case is gonna go today?"

"Hey... what do I look like, officer, an information booth, for crissakes? Go ask the prosecutor over there. Really, pal... nobody tells me nothin' around here."

"Okay. Excuse me. Are you the prosecutor, sir?"

"Yes, I am... what do you need?"

"I've got a subpoena here for this gas-station robbery. It says it's for today at nine o'clock and I've been here since then and this is the right room but I haven't heard anything about it and I wonder if I should stick around."

"Here, let me see that. You've been here since nine? Hell, it's almost noon now. Let's see. Wait a minute... I remember this case. One of the guys from felony division worked out something with the public defender on this. This guy pleaded out to get some kind of suspended sentence or probation or something. This case was finished up over a week ago. What are you doing here now?"

"Well, I've got that subpoena and I was afraid of being in contempt..."

"Oh. Somebody should have called you to let you know. Well, you can get out of here now anyway—all on company time, right?"

"I'm on midnight shift, sir."

"Well, look, officer... these things happen, you can't expect things to go right all the time. I mean, we're all in this together ... all on the same team, right?"

"Yes sir."

"All right, then. Go home. Get some sleep. Forget it."

"Right."

Twenty-Eight

WALTER HAD no way of knowing how hungry Alvin was. He had no way of knowing that Alvin and three other guys wanted to put together a cocaine deal so bad they would do anything to make it work. It wasn't a big coke deal by today's standards, but Alvin and his partners took it very seriously.

The only things Walter took seriously were the love for his wife and his undying belief that life was for having a good time. Not that he wasn't a good cop, I mean, he was out there every day, and when the radio sent him on a job he handled it. But for Walter the job was someplace he had to be, and while he was there he may as well have a good time. He was a prankster, a guy with a quick wit and sharp tongue. In briefing he always had a gag going or was harassing some new guy or a lieutenant to the delight of everyone. On the street with the public he was neat, courteous, professional, and efficient. He just didn't take it seriously.

Walter had no way of knowing that it was Alvin and his partners who had caused the manager at the seafood restaurant to set off the silent robbery alarm. The dispatcher advised the northend units of the alarm, and Walter drove his cruiser that way. Silent alarms went off all over town, every day, and most of the time there was a malfunction or some clerk had hit the button unknowingly, or some such silly thing. This was ten o'clock on a beautiful Sunday morning, and Walter still had parts of the morning newspaper scattered all over the front seat of his car. The city was starting to stretch and wake up, and it was hard to take a robbery alarm at a seafood restaurant seriously.

Walter had no way of knowing as he approached the restaurant that Alvin's partners had seen him coming and had driven off, leaving only Alvin still inside. Walter parked his cruiser on the north side of the building, grabbed his clipboard so he could record the pertinent information for his false-alarm report, got out, and walked easily into the restaurant through the kitchen door. Walter met Alvin in a small hallway leading out to the parking lot, Walter standing there with his pen in one hand and his clipboard in the other, and Alvin standing there with a cut-down .22 caliber rifle. A .22 caliber rifle is a small gun that shoots a small bullet, and as a high-noon weapon it's pretty hard to take seriously.

Alvin shot Walter three times with the .22, and as Walter went down Alvin ran past him and out into the parking lot to escape along with the others. He found that they had fled, and he knew more police officers would be along in seconds. He turned and ran back inside. Walter, laying huddled on the floor in the fetal position, helpless, managed to grip his radio and transmit, "Help me . . . help me, I've been shot." Those of us who heard those words, that voice on the radio, will never forget it. Most of us didn't recognize the voice, we only felt the terror and the pain. We heard it and we rushed headlong toward where it had to have come from, and we took it very seriously.

Alvin knelt beside Walter and demanded the keys to the police cruiser. Walter, through clenched teeth, told him which pants pocket to dig into. Alvin got the keys. Then he grabbed Walter's .38 service revolver, ripped it out of the holster, placed the barrel tight against Walter's head just behind the ear, and fired one shot into Walter's skull.

Alvin made his getaway in the police cruiser, and the first officers to arrive on the scene found Walter huddled on the ground, dead. There was the inevitable violent surge of police activity, and all four suspects were captured; two almost immediately, Alvin a week later, and the fourth some time after that. During questioning they admitted to attempting the robbery to generate funds for their cocaine deal. Walter was buried quietly with private services. The court system plodded along, and Alvin's three partners were convicted and given life sentences. Alvin was also convicted and sentenced to death. He sits on Florida's death row, and even though well-meaning or publicity-seeking lawyers have appealed his case every way there can be, his sentence still stands. The governor has signed the warrant, and every time it comes up the media gives us good coverage on those loudly opposed to the death penalty and on those unfortunates who live such a bleak existence on death row. We as a society take out our conscience and examine it closely, trying to assure ourselves of our morality and of the notion that we are in fact civilized.

Alvin has waited to die in the electric chair for over ten years. The latest ploy by those trying to save him describes him as being mentally ill. He sees space beings and talks with God and blinks his eyes. The court is pondering the question of whether we can put to death a man who is now insane, even though he was sane at the time of his crime and conviction. The sentence, however, still stands: he must die for what he did to Walter, his family, and all of us.

If it were possible, if it could be arranged, I would travel to where Alvin is today and I would watch as he was strapped into the chair, and I would pull the switch.

Seriously.

Twenty-Nine

"DAMN! LOOK who it is! How the hell are ya? Finally decided to come out into the night to a cop bar and mingle with your fellow soldiers manning the thin blue line."

"Yeah... I just needed to get out of the house for a while. You know how it is..."

"No shit I do. I know *exactly* how it is..."

"Pretty good crowd for the middle of the week, isn't it? I'm surprised... thought it would be quiet in here."

"Hell, this place is *always* busy. Look around at the chicks, will ya? One thing about this place, there's usually beaucoup pussy to be scoped, what with the ladies from records and the comm center, and the cop groupies and stuff."

"Uh, yeah."

"Man, a couple of these ladies have got the *look*, know what I mean? They want to feel more secure, so they take a cop to bed. Actually, who needs a bed? A cruiser in the back parking lot will do just fine if the damn seat will move back far enough to get out from under the steering wheel."

"Yeah. Damn, that first one went fast. Want another?"

"Sure. I'm tellin' ya... things start to get frosty at home, you hang around here, let one of these split-tail fans of ours latch on to you, and go home smelling like you been tuna-fishing. Fix you right up, and it doesn't hurt your perspective on things, either... reminds you that the old lady isn't the only one out here with a fuckin' vagina."

"Uh-huh..."

"What's the matter, man? You sound less than enthusiastic.

89

Oh, I know, you don't think you can score with any of these chicks. Shit, I can tell you of two that have already mentioned here and there that they'd like to see you twirl that nightstick of yours, dig it?"

"No...that's not it..."

"Wait a minute. Look right over there, past that eight-ball from the sheriff's office...see that little chick with the long reddish-brown hair? You've seen her up in records, I'm sure. She told a lady I know that you are a gentleman, and that turned her on. Look, she's lookin' over here."

"That's okay, man, I don't..."

"What's the deal, dude?"

"Shit, man...I'm *married.*"

"Jesus...is that it? *Most* of us are married at least once, you pinhead! What's that got to do with it? Nobody's talkin' about the love affair of all time here, we're talkin' about getting your knob polished, getting your tubes cleaned out by some sweet young thing that'll rock you till your skin turns red...no strings, no headaches."

"Uh-huh..."

"Listen, dude, a wise old veteran detective told me once that any cop that isn't gettin' a little pussy on the side is either a queer or a liar. Which one are you?"

"I'll tell you what, my man...it's gonna be hard for you to give anybody advice with your jaw wired shut..."

"Whoa, chill out, guy...don't get pissed. I'm just sayin' that you're no different than any of us. Things get weird at home, the old lady starts to look at you like you're the man from Mars, and you get out and get a quick taste of the forbidden fruit...does ya good."

"Yeah, I know. I don't mean to get pissed at you, it's just that I'm sort of confused right now. I don't know *what* the hell's goin' on at home, but it isn't good. My wife and I are beginning to look at each other like strangers, like I look at her and she still looks fine but there's no *feeling* and she looks back at me like I'm...I'm..."

"The north end of a southbound armadillo?"

"...yeah...or some guy she's living with, but can't remember why."

Pause.

"I don't know what's going to happen to us, and maybe you're right, about bein' out here and all..."

"Yeah...so this motorman, who will remain *unnamed*...stops this fine and very Palm Beachy lady in her drop-top "beamer" out on the strip there. Struts up, pencil in hand, she says the right things, and a few minutes later he's with her in a big house off Las Olas, in the bedroom. She's even *more* fine when she's naked and waiting, and our motorcycle hero is hopping around trying to get just as naked without catching his purple-headed diamond cutter in his zipper. Right?"

Grins, headshakes.

"Before he gets completely undone she has a request...could even be a demand. She wants him to leave his helmet and sunglasses on as he joins her on that bed...*and* his big shiny boots, too. This motorman stated later that it was good, but the horseshoe cleats on his heels made it hard to get any traction on the silk sheets."

Groans.

"So I'm brand new, out on the beach on midnight shift, and I see this car parked in the southbeach lot, down by the Yankee Clipper. I pull up, see only the driver, a guy, leaning back, his eyes closed. I slam my door as I get out, walk up, and oops... there's a chick with her face down in his lap. I begin to stammer and stutter and he just smiles and the chick looks up at me and when she does his tool sits right up there in front of her face. She has to look cross-eyed past it to see me as I say in my most pubescent official voice: 'What are you doing?' She sighes, pushes the pole out of the way with her nose, and says, 'I'm sucking his cock, you cretin.' Honesty has always been something I appreciate, so I left."

Someone gives a Bronx Cheer.

"Great stories, huh, guy? Ready for another...wait, here she comes, man..."

"Hello."

"Uh...hi."

"This must be my lucky night. I don't come here that often, and here I am tonight, and here *you* are. Maybe you'll say something to me besides asking for a vehicle registration or criminal background check on some maggot..."

"Well, you know...at work it's hard..."

"Other places too, I hope. Oh, I'm just kidding...I can't believe I said that. Guess I'm acting like a little girl with a crush, huh?"

"Would you like another beer?"

"You bet. So...are you out just to get out, or are you tired of being alone even when you're not?"

"Something like that. I don't know. Mostly I'm a straight-shooter I guess..."

"That's what I like about you. You're real, and all I hear about your work on the street is that you're an asskicker and a name-taker. Do you take telephone numbers too?"

"You've heard about the way I work on the street? That means something to you?"

"Yeah, it means something to me. You're a *cop*, you've got balls, and you do things the other pencilnecks I've known in my life wouldn't *think* of doing. Hell, the way you walk, the way you keep your face so serious all the time...it turns me on." Pause. "No kidding."

"What was that about your telephone number...?"

Thirty

"I'LL TELL you what really burns me up, officer. She only had the damn bike for about three weeks, less than a month, and it's already stolen. I know it's not gonna do any good to report it to you guys, but my wife insisted, so I'm doin' it. I wish you guys would patrol in this neighborhood more, we never see you guys. With the blacks moving in all around here now the place is changing, know what I mean, officer?"

I looked at him as he spoke the same old lines. A big man, with a red face and thinning blond hair. His forearms were sunburned and his old T-shirt was clean but frayed around the edges. He stood in his socks with me and his little girl in the front yard of his home. I looked at him and said, "It doesn't hurt to make a report. Sometimes we do find them abandoned, and if we have time we occasionally check a kid here or there riding down the street. It would have been better if you had the serial number written down somewhere, that way we can check it months later, even if the bike's been painted."

The big man looked at me and rubbed his hand across his face and shrugged his shoulders. He was a working man, and dealing with the police was new to him. I could tell he was uncomfortable as he gently patted his daughter on top of her head and said, "Yeah, well, we threw that serial number out somehow. We were hoping you could use the description of the bike, it's a real pretty bike, to sorta look around for it."

I looked down at the girl, who was standing slightly behind one of her father's legs, with her thin arms wrapped around his hips. She had blonde hair pulled back into two tight pony-tails, and she was wearing a Star Wars T-shirt and pink shorts. On her feet were pink plastic sandals. She peeked out from behind her father's leg, looked up at me, and said, "My daddy said right. It really is a pretty bike," and the tears started and her father looked embarrassed and smiled at me and it made me feel rotten so I said to her, "Well, in order for me to search for your bike I'll have to know all about it."

The little girl began in a small voice, "It's a Huffy bike, not too big." Her father cut in softly with, "Twenty inches." And she nodded and said, "It's a real nice pink color, with like knobby tires and high handlebars with pink streamers going out." I was officiously writing this down, and asked, "Is there anything else about it... anything special? What kind of seat?" She stepped away from her dad and spread her hands about two feet apart and said, "It's a long seat... and it goes like this," and she made a curve with one hand, "It's a little higher in the back than in the front, and it's pink with all different colored flowers stuck on it." I looked at the father again and said, "I would have to guess her favorite color is pink." He smiled and said, "Yeah... she always has liked pretty things like that. And she's my favorite little girl." When he said this she went back to his side and wrapped herself around his leg again and looked up at him and I could see he was always gentle with her and they were close and I wished I could go right to my car and pull another pink bike out of the trunk because I knew he had to work long and hard to buy her that bike and guessed he probably spent a lot of time worrying about keeping the bill collectors from his door. The whole thing bummed me out. I told them I would do my best and the big man said, "Thanks, officer," and they stood there in the yard as I drove off in my unit.

Less than ten minutes later I passed one of those little corner markets and looked over on the sidewalk and there, sitting right in front of the doors, was a twenty-inch Huffy with high bars and a banana seat. The bike was pink, there were pink streamers coming from the handgrips, and it had a multitude of colored flowers stuck all over the pink seat. Bingo, I thought, and pulled into the lot just as two little black kids came out of the store and went to the bike. The girl was slightly older than the boy. She had springy hair plaited into those tight corn-rows with the rows getting bigger toward the back of her head. She was wearing a striped T-shirt and blue pants, with blue sneakers on her feet. She was carrying a quart of milk in a bag and as she got on the bike she turned and said to the little boy, "Here, Jimmy. You hang onto this milk, and don't be wigglin' around so much back there." The little boy, who was wearing a red buttoned shirt with the tails out over his gray shorts, with no shoes, took the milk and said, "You just be drivin' the bike." Then as I approached I heard him mumble under his breath, "I hate big sisters."

She looked at him hard and swung her leg over the seat and they both froze and looked at me with big eyes and little round mouths when I said, "Hold it a minute, little girl."

I stood with my hands on my hips, towering over them, gazing down into their scared and confused faces. Neither one moved or even breathed until I said, "Hey ... relax ... I just want to look at your bicycle a minute." The girl swung her leg back off the seat and stood there holding the handlebars. The boy eased himself off and stood clutching the milk against his chest ... still staring at me wide-eyed.

I slowly walked all the around them, and as I did nothing moved but their eyes. I looked the bike over; it matched the description perfectly. I looked at the girl and said, "How long have you had this bike?" She looked quickly at her brother, then back at me, "Long time." The boy backed up a little and shrugged his shoulders, so I asked again, "C'mon now ... how long have you had this bike?" The boy stayed quiet but the girl put her head down, stuck out her lower lip, and mumbled, "Bout two days ... but it's mine." "Now listen," I said, "I'm looking for a bike just like this that another little girl told me was stolen from her, so I have to check this bike out real good. Can you tell me where you got the bike?"

The little girl slowly put the kickstand down, stepped back, folded her arms across her chest, put her chin up, stuck her lip out farther, and said, "My daddy bought me this here bike. My daddy bought it for me and he didn't steal it and that other little girl done tol' you wrong." I scratched my head and sighed, "Well, I'll have the other girl meet us here and look at this bike and maybe we can clear this up, okay?"

As I spoke into the radio, telling the dispatcher to contact the reportee I heard the girl tell her brother, "Jimmy . . . you run home and tell momma what be happenin' here . . ." The boy took off like a shot, holding the milk like he was Herschel Walker, shirt-tails flying in the breeze. Now it was just me and the little girl, but she was still holding her ground. "So whatchu gonna do when that other little girl gets here? What's she gonna tell you 'bout this bike? Huh?" I said quietly, "I don't know, honey. Maybe it has a special mark on it somewhere that she can identify. I'm just trying to find her stolen bike, that's all." She glared at me and looked at the bike. I watched the girl's lower lip begin to quiver as the dispatcher told me the others were on the way. I felt uncomfortable standing there with the girl, so I turned the bike over to follow procedure and read the serial number off the frame to the records dispatcher just to see if it was in the system. I was advised the check would take a few minutes.

As I finished an old white Chevy pulled into the lot and out jumped the little blonde girl and her big father. She stayed close to him as they approached and I heard her say to him, "He found it, daddy!" The little black girl backed up against the newspaper machines as they got closer, and then there was a few seconds of everybody just quietly staring at each other. Finally the silence was broken by the big man who said softly, "Well, officer, that sure looks like the bike all right." The little black girl began to cry softly as the white girl slowly walked around the bike, touching it.

Before I could say anything else a deep voice said, "Hey,

officer, what's going on here?" We all turned to see a small wiry black man standing on the sidewalk. He spoke again and I was surprised to hear that deep melodious voice coming out of his hard little body. "My boy came after me. Says my little girl is in some kind of trouble. Is she?" I looked at him. He was only about five-six, maybe a hundred and twenty pounds. He wore a clean white T-shirt and dark green work pants. He had on a pair of beat-up construction boots that were unlaced. His hair was cut very close to his skull and I could see that when he smiled it would be a full smile full of big white even teeth. His skin was the color of oiled wood. His hands were big and his arms lean but well-developed. In the skin of his hands and forearms was the shadow of white powdered dust...concrete. He probably threw block or mixed mud, and although he and the other father would never pass and wave on the street I knew immediately that he had been working hard all of his life, cared greatly for his family, worried about paying his bills, and was as good to his kids as life would let him be. Just like the other guy.

The little black girl ran to her father, wrapped herself around his legs, and said, "That po-lice said the bike is stolen, daddy. Tell him you bought it for me, daddy. Tell him." The black man looked at me and nodded. "My little girl didn't steal that bike, officer." I watched as he straightened his back and lifted his chin up and I knew he was used to talking to people always taller than him and always in a superior position to him. I replied, "Wait. No one is accusing your daughter of stealing this bike. These people reported a bike like this stolen from them a couple of days ago, I saw this bike and it matches the description they gave me so I asked these people to come over and take a closer look so we could straighten this matter out."

He looked at me and I could see that old look in his eyes that said whenever the police straightened matters out it usually meant the black man was going to get the short end of the stick. He put his hand on the bike seat and said, "I bought this bike, officer." "Where?" I asked, and he went on, "I bought it over to the K-mart there, officer." "Well, how about a receipt, then?" He stuck his hands in his pocket and said quietly, "I don't have no receipt, officer."

While this was going on I saw the little white girl talking softly to her father, who asked, "Are you sure, honey?" and I saw her shake her head yes and turn away with tears in her eyes. The big man cleared his throat, straightened up, pulled the bottom of his T-shirt down over his middle, and said, "Uh, officer... I really appreciate you tryin' to find the bike, but my little girl here says this isn't her bike after all." The black girl's face brightened and the black man stared quietly at the big white man as I asked, "Are you sure? This bike fits the description of the stolen one. How does she know for sure?" He gently put one hand on his daughter's shoulder and pulled her to him. She was crying pretty good now. He reached out with one huge arm, picked the bike up by the back of the seat, and said, "My little girl loves pink things, and one of her favorite TV characters is that Miss Piggy, I mean, she just loves that show and all. We got her a kit that has those Muppets on these little decals and she stuck that Miss Piggy almost everywhere, even got yelled at by her ma for puttin' one on the TV set. She says she stuck a couple under the seat and onto the back fender here... and you can look at this bike and see that they aren't there. Even if they'd been scraped off you would still be able to tell. Besides, officer, I forgot to tell you before but those knobby tires she had were whitewalls... and these ain't."

He slowly put the bike back down and we all stood there in silence, staring at the back fender. The black girl's face showed hope and her father's face disbelief as I prepared to apologize for causing an uncomfortable situation. Before I could say anything the records dispatcher came blaring across the radio and told me the bike serial number I had given her to check was listed as stolen. I read the number back and she confirmed it again and then I said, "Can you give me any details?" She came back with, "Ten-four... this serial number is listed to one of about twenty that were taken two weeks ago in a business burglary in Wilton Manors. The shop had all the numbers, and

Wilton Manors PD has been telexing everybody to look out for them. Most have been recovered locally. This is an active case, and they request that any officer finding one of the bikes get the details and bring the bike into evidence. They advise they *will* pick up all recovered bikes." I asked her to stand by, looked at the black man, and said, "No receipt? And you bought it at the K-mart?"

I saw him look at his daughter for a second and I could see the pain in his eyes as he said, "Well, I said I bought it over to the K-Mart...but it was alongside there. These young guys had a big truck and they was sellin' them there. I paid a good amount of money, officer. They didn't give no receipts but there was a lot of men there buyin' things and everything was new and I didn't think it was stolen. I really didn't." I could see that he wanted to tell us that no matter how hard he worked his whole life he could never buy the family he loved the things he wanted for them because of his wages. He wanted to tell us that life was hard and that he was hard, and that he had been breaking his ass every day his whole damn life and no matter how hard he tried he always came up short and how just once he wanted to do something nice for his daughter, just once he would like to break even. But he was a proud man, so he simply said, "I didn't know it was stolen, officer."

I looked at him and the white guy, and sighed. Both little girls were standing behind their dads now, both crying and pulling at the cloth of their father's work trousers. The big guy put one hand on his daughter's shoulder and turned her toward his car, saying, "C'mon honey, let's go home now, okay?" The black man rubbed his hand across his head, hard, put one hand softly on top of his daughter's curls, and said gently, "Hey there, button-nose...don't be cryin' like that. Let's go home and tell momma what happened. C'mon now, honey..."

The white man and his daughter got into their old car and drove off, and the black man and his daughter turned and walked to the corner of the building, stepped down into the broken glass and bent beer cans, and walked out of sight... leaving me standing there alone with the little pink bike.

Thirty-One

YOU HAVE to wonder about the almost implacable normality that can be maintained by a trapped audience. As one of the first officers responding to the report of a woman choking in a restaurant, I wondered what it must have been like for her, struggling for life in the midst of those who saw her predicament as an infringement on social decorum . . .

She sat nicely at one of the better tables. Her hair and makeup were just right, and she wore a lovely dress that wasn't, you know, too fancy. She was with a pleasant group, but looked down with some misgivings at the large steak on her plate. She knew she shouldn't have ordered it, she always had trouble with her dentures. Even though she really loved steak, chewing it hurt her so bad she couldn't enjoy it. Oh well, it looked so good. She'd just take bigger bites and try not to chew it much.

"So whatdya say? Want a drink before dinner?"

"Hey, waitress, can we have some water, please?"

"No . . . I'm serious. Coquilles Saint Jacques is much too rich. How about a shrimp cocktail?"

"I'm tellin' you right now, Harry . . . s'cuse me, could you pass the butter? Thanks. The damn Dolphins just aren't that good . . . they won't make it."

She sat with her hands in her lap, trying to use her tongue and throat muscles to help her bring the big piece of steak back up from her throat. She had chewed politely until it hurt too bad, then she had swallowed. At that moment she realized she had made a mistake. Her throat locked around the meat and it sat there blocking her breathing, choking her.

How embarrassing.

Now she tried to swallow harder, hoping no one at the table could see what she was doing. Of course she could just reach in with her fingers and push it in, or pull it out, or something, but my God... how would *that* look? She tried to swallow again, and felt the pain.

"Good evening, my name is Lance and I'll be your server tonight. Jimmy there will assist me, so ask either one of us if you need anything, all right?"

"C'mon, try one of these muffins, they're really good."

"Our special tonight is the stuffed grouper. Of course it's fresh daily, and it comes with your choice of baked potato or rice pilaf."

"It's not that I don't find you attractive, Mr. Steadman. It's just that... I don't know, I think having a relationship with your boss can be awkward, you know?"

Finally she could stand it no more. She had to have air, she had to breathe. She grabbed her throat with her hands and tried to breathe in and out as hard as she could. She began to gag and looked up horrified at the others around the table. She saw they were staring at her, and she was mortified.

"God... did you hear that? Someone's sick."

"Yeah... I think it's someone over at that other table."

"No honey, it's red wine with meat, white with fish..."

"Oh I'm sorry, sir... I thought Lance was getting your bread for you."

She struggled for air, not caring how she looked. She couldn't breathe! She became tense, shoving her chair away from the table violently and trying to cough. Her throat muscles tightened more, and as she panicked she fought harder against herself, still not breathing. She felt an immense pain in her chest, and as she slid off the chair and fell to the floor she saw the people at her table staring open-mouthed.

"What's that commotion over there?"

"Oh, somebody probably had too much to drink."

"Uh ... my wife is sure this fish is spoiled. It tastes slightly funny to me, too. Could you take this back and recommend something else?"

"Look. It's really not that difficult. So I'm your boss, so what? I'm just a man, and you're a woman, and we work together and I'm around you all the time and I'm attracted to you. There's no reason in the world we can't enjoy each other and still be professional at the office."

"You mean you're gonna leave the rest of that veal?"

Her ears were filled with a roaring sound, and she felt the rough carpet against her cheek. She felt the tears running down her face and wondered where her purse was.

"Hey ... there's a cop running in here. And look, a couple of those medical rescue people ..."

"Yeah, some drunk must have slipped against the urinal."

"No sir, if you get the surf and turf it comes with a strip steak, and the lobster is a *little* different than if you order a lobster dinner."

"George. Get the rice instead of the potato."

The pain in her chest was unbearable, and she tried to cry out but couldn't. Then she felt rough hands digging in her mouth, and in her throat. My God! Her dentures were gone! She turned her head and vomited, and as she fell into confused unconsciousness her bowels loosened, and she was ashamed.

"Ugh ..."

"Don't look. Uh, just don't look over there ..."

"God ... I knew this was a bad table ..."

"I'll bet she ordered that Co-keel Saint stuff you told us about, ha, ha, ha ..."

"The Vikings? You gotta be kidding. Here, let me have some of that cake. The Vikings ... when was the last time they did anything like a real team?'"

"I swear I couldn't eat another bite ..."

"How is everything here, okay? Oh, that? Apparently an older lady is having a problem. I think they're going to take her to be checked or something. What? I thought *Jimmy* was bringing your bread!"

"Of course we have desert... I'll bring you the menu..."

She was unconscious and couldn't know it but they wiped the mess from her face, placed an oxygen mask over her mouth, gave her an injection, did external heart massage on her chest, rolled her onto a stretcher, covered her with a sheet, and carried her through the crowd and out to the waiting ambulance. On the floor was the mess where she had been, including a thick piece of steak almost four inches long.

"Guess it's about time they carried that old broad outta here ... you'd think they could move faster with all the money they make nowadays."

"Well honey, I told you not to look over there. They'll clean it up. C'mon... what would you like to drink?"

"Betty said her lobster was tough, and I noticed Sam just picked at his chicken, and I *know* that fish was frozen. Next time let's go back out to the Raintree."

"Geeze... will you look at this bill?"

"No. Now listen... last time we all went out you grabbed the check. This time it's on me."

"So what if the waiter was gay, Harry? The service was good, and on TV they said you couldn't catch anything from them..."

"I did not leave her too much of a tip, honey, and she was not making eyes at me. I left what I thought was fair. Honey? Honey..."

"Well, okay, Mr. Steadman, one drink at your place, but I really can't stay... I have to go to *work* tomorrow..."

"You can be late! See, this is a good deal for you already!"

"I thought the dinner was lousy. Who could enjoy it with all that commotion?"

"Can we stop for some Alka Seltzer on the way home?"

"Wonder what happened to that old broad anyway?"

Thirty-Two

WHEN I had been on the department four or five years they began hiring females and putting them through the academy to be assigned to road patrol. Those were the old days, so there were only a couple of women on the job, and they worked with the detective division, with juveniles or rape cases. Very traditional. I was feeling salty by now, and the thought of females ... girls ... treading the all-male domain of the street didn't sit well with me. I believed at that time it was a silly experiment forced on us by the courts, and that the shiny new lady cops would see some shit on the street, get their asses kicked, and go back to more "female" jobs. I was a dinosaur.

I was also a professional, and took administrative decisions as they came down. I kept that attitude when working with the new lady cops. I stayed aloof, tried not to patronize them or overreact to their needs, and shared my experience when they'd let me. I believe all the male cops in my squad listened a little harder to the radio when we heard a female get a call, and sort of leaned that way in case something went down "they couldn't handle." Conversely, when one of them backed us up we strutted around, waved off any suggestion that we needed help, and, if the shit hit the fan, hoped one of the *guys* was on his way.

One of the first ones to come out of the academy was a little thing with long strawberry-blonde hair, a trim figure, and great smile. She was fresh and pleasant and outgoing and fun. She smelled good, and was very friendly. Most of us crusty cops had to admit having her in the middle of a coffee-and-doughnut session was like a breath of fresh air... and *man*, you should have heard the hair-raising and heroic stories she had to listen to! One thing I noticed about her that I wasn't comfortable with was her eagerness to be accepted. She didn't make the mistake of trying to be just like us... there were other females who used the foul language and tried to strut like we did, but it just didn't play, you know? This lady stayed very feminine and sweet, but she literally hung on the guys... she was a toucher, her hand was always on somebody's shoulder or arm. Too close for comfort.

One day I was doing some paperwork in the write-up room. Write-up was a small room behind briefing stuffed with typewriters, forms, phone books, and a telephone. Our good deeds were dutifully recorded there, and it could be a small purgatory for cops who had to struggle with written words and numbered spaces to stuff them into. On that day there was no one in the room but myself and this new female cop. I was busy, and was not paying attention to what she was doing. As I stood and bent to pick up the work I had had just finished she passed behind me, grabbed the cheek of my butt with one hand, slapped it, and walked off, saying, "How's it going out there today, Mac?"

She walked to the far wall without waiting for an answer and reached for the phone. As she did I was right behind her, and with my right hand I reached out and grabbed a whole *handful* of her tush. I deliberately grabbed much more than she had, to the point where she was almost on her toes as she gasped and swung around.

First her right hand came whistling toward my face, the palm open. I grabbed her wrist with my left hand. Immediately her left came from the other side, and I stopped it with my right. I turned my hips just as her knee came up, as I knew it would. Then I squeezed with my hands and held her tight. She struggled, her face very red and her eyes wide in anger. Neither one of us spoke for a moment, locked in a silent struggle, our faces inches apart, our hot breaths mixing in front of us. She was very strong, but so was I, and the more she struggled the more pressure I applied. I didn't know how long it could go on, so finally I pushed her back against the counter and wall as I released her and stepped back myself.

Quietly, I said, over her heavy breathing. "You want to do the same job I do out there on the street? Prove it to me *out there*. None of the guys I work with grab me on the ass, and I give them the same courtesy. We can be cops together, you and me, and I'll back you just like I would any other cop... but you don't touch me, and I won't touch you. Got it?"

We stared at each other, both tense, both pissed... her cheeks were fiery red and her eyes flashed. I turned and walked out of the room.

That lady cop turned out to be one of the good ones, eventually became a streetwise veteran, and made promotion. She and I never spent any time off the job together, but on the job we became friends, sharing assignments, squad cars, and patrol zones through the various shifts. I learned she could be counted on in the clutch, she was smart enough to know the laws and the rules, and she carried herself on the job as a professional and off the job as a lady. I liked her.

I had been wrong about female cops.

Thirty-Three

I WENT through the academy with both of these guys. One was a curly-headed, big-mouthed Irish kid. He had buckteeth and a bushy mustache, and he told outrageous stories about when he had been an MP in Vietnam. Most of us forgave his tales because it was obvious he was trying so hard to be liked and accepted. He wasn't a bad guy: he just tried too hard.

The other guy was what we perceived as a typical New Yorker. We told him so all the time, and he loved it. He was proud to be Jewish, and he loved the fact that he was going to be a Jewish cop. Very intelligent, but a wiseguy... always with the right answer. Pushy, loud, but nice. He looked at me like I was some kind of deprived orphan child when I confessed to being unfamiliar with kosher food. Ah, that food he could talk about all day long. We were always going to get together someday and he was going to introduce my ignorant palate to all the Jewish foods. He could make lunch sound like a spiritual experience.

The Irish kid would hold up the class asking dumb questions or making a remark about how he had seen the same thing in the war zone. The Jewish guy would hold up the class by arguing with the instructor over a small point of law, or zinging someone with a joke.

A year later both of these guys died chasing a young black purse-snatcher.

A real rainy day. They were riding together in an unmarked car. The black kid grabbed the purse and jumped into his car and skidded out of the shopping center lot. The Irish kid and the Jewish guy in their Plymouth chased the black kid in his Chevy.

A rainy curve . . . way too fast.

The black kid lost control of his car but recovered enough to drive off into the mist. The other two kids lost control and impacted a huge tree so hard it killed them both instantly.

We were all young then, in many ways, and it was "rough." A "real bad break," a "raw deal," a "shame . . . really." We were stunned, saddened, and angry. Guys actually died doing what we did . . . it was The Real Thing.

Everybody eventually learned who the black kid was. We had the car identified, no doubt in our minds. But we couldn't prosecute him. The old lady who lost her purse was the only witness, an ineffective one, and the case hinged on her identifying the suspect. We knew who he was, but we couldn't nail him. Ten years later I still remember his name. I vowed to kill him if I ever got the chance. I stopped him in his Chevy one night and told him so, but I couldn't tell if I made an impression or not. Don't know where he is now . . . jail maybe, or dead.

Maybe he's one of the statistics of high murder rates among young black males.

The Irish kid and the Jewish guy died.

For the cause, for justice, for the defense of the rights of all people . . . for the twenty-three dollars in the old lady's purse.

Thirty-Four

IT WAS late afternoon, getting on toward early evening. I was hot, tired, irritable, and impatient for the shift to end so I could go home. I cruised southbound on Fourth Avenue, killing time, waiting, hoping the dispatcher would not call me at the last minute and send me on some stupid call like larceny hubcaps or parking lot fender-bender.

I sat through the red light at Seventeenth Street and then continued southbound slowly. I watched as an old station wagon pulled out from a side street two blocks ahead of me. The car slowly wandered across all three lanes, stayed in the center for a while, then drifted back to the curb lane. Now what the hell? I watched the driver turn his head back and forth, moving his shoulders, looking through the windshield and both side windows. I watched the brake lights come on, then off, then on again. I hung back, thinking, *shit*, as the car again swerved from one lane to the other and back again.

I have to have a drunk driver bumping along Fourth Avenue in broad daylight ? Now?

I eased my unit up behind the wagon and turned on my flashing red and blue lights to initiate a traffic stop. The wagon kept going, weaving along, the driver looking everywhere but behind him. We drove our little parade like that for a block, and then I began hitting the siren, on and off . . . I just blooped the siren, trying to get the guy's attention. Nothing. He just kept scanning the area, and the wagon continued to slide over whatever lane it happened to drift into.

109

I had been a cop for years and I thought I was pretty hot. Hot, cynical, impatient, intolerant, target-oriented, and very hard. I had been behind this guy now for several blocks, all lights flashing, siren whooping, horn blowing, and he had completely ignored me. He had not stopped, he had not pulled over to be arrested. He had just driven on like I didn't exist.

Wrong.

He pulled into the left-turn lane at State Road 84 and was caught there by the light. Now, Mr. DWI . . . now you gonna meet Officer Friendly. I pulled right up behind him, lights still flashing, jumped out of my unit and stalked up the side of his car, stopping just to the rear of the driver's door. The window was rolled up and I looked in to see a man in his early fifties, balding, with leathery sunburned skin. He wore work pants and a checked flannel shirt. He sat there with his head down, rubbing his forehead.

I spread my legs, put my hands on my hips, and said, "Hey." Nothing.

I said, "Hey" again, and the man still sat there rubbing his head.

Remember I mentioned I had become an impatient cop? I stood there glaring down at this guy now and had already used most of it up. I was getting tired of this jerk not responding to my signals. What a dimbulb, must be drunk on his ass.

"Hey, pal!" I yelled, and hit the window several times with my fist. Then I pounded on his door and was preparing to grab the door handle, open the door, and rip the guy out onto the pavement, when he turned, looked up at me, and stared open-mouthed.

"Don't just sit there, man . . . get outta the car!" I yelled.

The guy looked at me, confused, fumbled for the window crank, and rolled the window down. Then he sat there with an agitated, questioning look. His eyes were clear, and I did not smell the odor of an alcoholic beverage on his breath. But he was definitely uncomfortable or confused, or something. And he sat there.

I grabbed the door handle now, motioning him out with one

hand while I shouted, "C'mon, pal... out of the car!" He stared
and shook his head and I yelled, "Move it! You got a driver's
license? Break it out!" He looked back over his shoulder at my
car, then at me, shook his head, and reached for the door handle.
He opened the door, turned his body, and slowly began to exit
from behind the wheel.

I stood there watching him on the balls of my feet, wired
now. I was through waiting for this dude. He was taking all
day to get out of the car, and he hadn't even started to drag out
his wallet and hunt for his DL. The end of the damn shift, the
end of the damn day, and I have to deal with a DWI. A minimum
of one hour, paperwork and all... and he moved so slowly and
looked so confused and if he didn't improve real quick I was
going to jerk him out of his shoes, move him back to my unit
with his feet never touching the ground, and stuff him into the
backseat. He could be confused on his way to jail. The more I
watched him the more angry I became. All of the day's agitation
and frustration came welling up inside me. I felt my chest
tightening, my arms harden, my hands turn to fists. I coiled
on the balls of my feet, tightened, and prepared to launch myself
at the man.

The man stared at me and I saw the fear in his eyes, and
then his hand shot back into his hip pocket, grabbed something,
and started out. I saw the movement and instinctively jumped
back, turned my body, and felt my hand on the grips of my
revolver. With one hand the man whipped out a small notebook,
with the other, a pen.

What?

The man flipped open the notebook, scribbled something,
ripped out the page, and handed it to me.

I read, *Can you help me? I need help.*

I was still up there, wired and ready to jump. Now I had to
stop and read this man's little note and pull myself back from
the brink.

I took a couple of deep breaths, looked at the guy, and asked,
"What's the matter with you, mister? What do you need?" He
looked at me, squinted, shook his head, and began writing

again. As he handed me the paper this time it began to finally dawn on me and I got a sick feeling in the pit of my stomach . . . realizing how close I had come.

Deaf. I'm deaf. Please look right at me when you speak. Please speak slowly—I'm upset.

I looked at the crumpled paper, rubbed a hand over my eyes, and felt nauseous.

My daughter. My youngest daughter. 14 years old. We fought, she and my wife, then me and her. Stupid fight about a school dance. She ran out the door, ran off. She's a good girl. Help me find her before it gets dark.

I took the third note and read it while he hastily scribbled another. He was intense, hunched over the little notebook, writing furiously. I felt drained, and somehow grateful.

She's wearing jeans and a red top. Long brown hair. Pretty. Not been out much after dark without us. She's deaf too.

I added that note to the others in my hand, looked at him, and spoke slowly, "I'll help you. Let's get out of this traffic. Follow me." He nodded and gave me a worried little smile. I smiled back weakly.

He followed me slowly up the block and into the cemetery entrance. I wanted a full description before I got the search going. I knew this didn't qualify as a missing person yet, and I knew that kids younger than his were out at night all the time, but I really wanted to help this guy. I advised the dispatcher and asked for more units to respond.

I parked on the drive and the man parked his wagon behind me. We got out and walked toward each other. He wrote as he walked. We were almost together when he looked up past my shoulder and his eyes lit up. He ripped the page out of the book, stuffed it into my hand, and hurried past me. I turned and saw the girl sitting in the shadow of a huge banyan tree. Her head was down and her long hair hung over her shoulders. I looked at the last note in my hand.

She's a good girl really. Deaf. A good girl. If anything happened to her . . .

I watched as the man knelt down in front of the girl and she looked up at him. He put one hand out and brushed the hair from her face. I watched as they held each other, the girl's shoulders heaving and the man's hand gently patting her back.

I got back into my unit quietly and drove around the drive, out of the cemetery, and toward the station. I folded all the little notes neatly and slid them into one of the pockets of my brief-case.

They stayed there, small but rich slices of humble pie, and shards of a window to another reality.

Thirty-Five

UNARMED BLACK YOUTH KILLED
BY OFF-DUTY COP
Suspect Shot In Back Fleeing
Attempted Robbery

LEROY CAME to Fort Lauderdale from Philadelphia to stay with his aunt. He was twenty-one years old and on parole from an armed robbery conviction. Leroy was very black and very big. He had intimidated people with his size and his blackness since his early teens. He became part of the criminal element early in life, and by the time he moved to Lauderdale he already had five convictions for felonies, assault, rape, and robbery.

I was off that day, and had been out fishing with friends. My wife was out of town on some trip with a college group, so I had come home to two noisily hungry cats. I decided to go down the street to get something to eat—for them and for me.

Leroy spent what money he had that afternoon drinking and getting high on some pills he bought from some dude on the corner. Then he went for a walk, looking, looking. He found a small rental-referral office on Davie Boulevard. The only person there was a young girl. Leroy was wearing sandals, black socks, and red jogging shorts.

Wait. There was one other thing.

Wrapped around his right hand, covering it completely to the wrist, was a dark green towel.

Leroy brought his sweating rubbery bulk into the office, pointed his right fist at the girl's face, supported his right wrist with his left hand, and said, "I've got a gun in here . . . give me the money." The girl, terrified, stammered that there was no money, it was only a referral office. Leroy looked around and then pointed at the girl's purse. She grabbed it and pulled out a couple of dollars and some change and dropped it onto her desk. Leroy looked at it, then back at her and said, "Now you have to kiss me . . ." The girl looked at his eyes, saw the hunger, the violence, and turned and fled to the bathroom where she slammed the door shut and locked it. She heard Leroy pounding on the door and then rummaging around in the office. She thought she heard the front door open, and then it was quiet. She waited a few moments, peered out, and saw that he was gone. She ran to the phone, but she called her boss, not the police.

I came out of the convenience store off Davie Boulevard with a bag of cat food, saw a Kentucky Fried Chicken place, and decided to go there and get a take-out dinner.

As I pulled into the parking lot I remembered it was dinnertime, Friday evening. The place was crowded with cars and people moving in and out of the lot and lobby of the restaurant. The traffic was heavy on the roadways with everyone getting off work and trying to get home. I parked and locked the car. I always locked my car because even when off duty I carried my gun and radio with me. I left them in the car and walked into the lobby of the place wearing a pair of ragged shorts, an old T-shirt, and sandals.

Once inside I got in line with about a dozen other people, all waiting their turn. The young girls working behind the counter were fast and efficient, and the line moved along well. I looked at the people while I waited, like I always did. It was the usual mix of old and young, men and women. Workers. I saw a big black guy three or four people back from the front of the line, talking with a long-haired white guy. I couldn't hear what was being said but apparently the long-hair had somehow rebuffed the black guy, who appeared agitated. I took a closer look at the black guy. Even though the lobby was air-conditioned his skin was covered with a sheen of sweat. He was very nervous, not standing still, and looking all around the room constantly. His eyes didn't look right to me at all, somehow distant and intense at the same time.

I had too many confrontations behind me, too many suspicious guys, too many arrests. Too many times my senses had said, "Trouble," and they were right. I watched the guy while he shuffled and jerked and moved his eyes and licked his lips and I thought, *shit.*

After the white dude refused to let him hold a dollar Leroy told him he'd better not stand too close to him when he got to the register. The white dude backed off and Leroy just kicked back, waiting. Finally it was his turn and the little girl behind the counter looked up at him and asked, "Can I help you, sir?"

I stood in line nervously as I watched the black guy play with the green towel wrapped around his right hand. He kept adjusting it, tightening it, holding it. Was it a bandage? Was it just to wipe his face? Was there something under the towel in his fist?

I watched and heard the girl ask, "Can I help you, sir?" and was stunned along with everyone else when Leroy pointed his right fist, wrapped in the towel, at the girl's face, supported his right wrist with his left hand, and said loudly, "It's a gun . . . give me all the money!" I stared. People froze and then began getting down, crouching under the tables. Leroy's whole body was tense, rigid. He leaned forward slightly and said, "Give me all the money . . . now!"

My mind was churning. I couldn't believe what I was seeing . . . the stupid sonofabitch was holding the place up in broad daylight in front of God and everybody! In front of *me*. It couldn't be happening, but it was. After the initial shock settled I reverted to what I was: cop.

I studied the situation technically, unemotionally, carefully. This dude was big and heavy, and I suspected he was spaced out on something. Big enough, tough enough, bad enough to pull an armed robbery now, here. He told us all he had a gun under that towel, and the way he was holding it and pointing it convinced me. I was standing there in my shorts, unarmed. I was tough, I knew it, but I weighed 155. Could I hurt him or contain him quickly enough? What if we struggled and the gun went off, what if the bullet hit someone in the crowded room?

What if he got pissed and began shooting while I stood there trying to make up my mind?

The girl began backing away from the counter, and Leroy leaned closer and tried to grab her. Then he started pounding on the cash register with his left hand. I had seen enough and had made up my mind. I had to get outside, get my gun and radio, and be ready when Leroy came out the door.

I stood directly behind Leroy as he stood at the counter. I turned slowly to my right and began walking softly toward the glass doors. I tried to will myself from Leroy's awareness. I knew one of the basic rules of robbery: Nobody leaves until it's over. As I pushed open the doors and stepped through I could feel him turning, screaming at me to stop, shooting me in the back as I tried to walk out in the middle of his robbery. I could feel the spot on my back where the hot bullet would rip into me. But he didn't, and it didn't, and I got outside, closed the door gently, and ran to my car, running out of my sandals on the way.

Now the frenzy, now the terror, now the exhilaration.

I couldn't work fast enough. I jammed the key in the lock, opened the door, and grabbed my gun and radio from under the seat. I turned the radio on and screamed, "Robbery in progress! Send me a backup!" I gave the location, threw the radio down and looked over my shoulder to see a commotion in the lobby. Then the glass doors slammed open and out he came.

Now the confusion, now the fear, now the chaos.

People in cars, on foot, in the lot, on the street, alongside the building, all stared open-mouthed when I screamed, "Everybody get down! Get down!" and ran toward Leroy, My gun held forward in my left hand. Leroy saw me coming, hesitated, then started running to my right, toward the back of the building. Behind him was a solid brick wall. Wrapped around his right hand was the towel.

Cars were parked nose-in along the building. As Leroy ran between the front of the cars and the wall I paralleled him behind the cars, with the lot to my back. I began yelling,

"Stop! Halt! I'm a police officer!"

"Freeze! Freeze, you sonofabitch! Hold it, asshole! Freeze!"

"I'm a *cop,* asshole!"

"Stop or I'll shoot! Stop or I'll shoot!"

"Stop, nigger, or I swear I'll fucking kill you!"

"I said *freeze!*"

Each time I yelled at him Leroy turned his body as he ran. When he turned his right hand pointed at me. His right hand held the gun under the towel, and he pointed it at me. Each time he turned I knew I should shoot him. I knew he would shoot me and I knew I had to shoot him. But I didn't. Behind him was that solid wall. All around us were people, screaming and running and diving to the ground. I very clearly saw a woman calmly shepherding two small children behind a car. I was afraid to shoot and miss, afraid of my bullets ricocheting off that wall and into the people. I was afraid Leroy would shoot and miss, or shoot and hit.

I was afraid.

I screamed at him because I wanted him to see me, to hear me, to know I was there. I was afraid, and I knew in my heart then that someone was going to die.

Leroy looked at me, he saw me running there, saw me pointing my revolver at him. He heard me, he heard me calling for him to stop, that I was a cop. But he just ran.

I paralleled Leroy until he reached the end of the building. Then I stopped as he turned at an angle, left, away from me and into the rear area of the building. As he turned from me I could see there were two places for him to go. If he angled more right he would come to a small alley that ran east from the rear of the place, along the rear fence of some neighboring businesses. If he stayed at the angle he was moving he would come to a small alcove at the end of a breezeway that was part of a highway motel located on the other side of the chicken place.

I couldn't let Leroy make it to either one.

I had been a cop too long to chase an armed felon down a blind alley alone. It would be too easy for him to ambush me in several ways. I would not do it.

Standing in the alcove at the end of the breezeway was a small gaggle of women and children, maybe half a dozen. I don't know what they were doing there. I pictured Leroy, running from an armed robbery with his gun, with a cop on his ass, grabbing one of the women or children as hostage. I would not let him.

I stopped running. I relaxed. I took a two-handed grip on my service revolver and I aimed it at the small of Leroy's back. I could see him very clearly along the length of the barrel. I could see his sweaty back, his creased neck, his arms pumping. I could see the elastic band in his red jogging shorts.

I squeezed the trigger and felt the gun jump in my hands.

Leroy fell face down, hard. He fell like someone had taken an invisible baseball bat and hit him in the ankles as he ran. He pitched forward and belly-flopped into the grass. Then he was still.

Then the silence. Then the long sigh. Then the screaming.

People ran and hid. People yelled and pointed, stared at me, and Leroy. People backed away, and came running. A woman brought me my radio and I spoke. Cops came. Crime Scene. Detectives. Sergeant, Lieutenant. Medical Rescue.

When the first backup guys arrived we approached Leroy slowly. His arms were flung away from his sides. His left hand was a fist. His right hand was still covered with the towel. We grabbed his ankles and rolled him over onto his back. He took one of those long dry breaths, you know, that last one.

Then he was dead.

I opened his hands. Slowly I unwrapped the towel from around his right hand. Under it was nothing. There was no gun, nothing. I opened his left fist. In his palm was a dime.

Later, much later, after my trial by newspaper, an investigation by the department, the state attorney's office, and the grand jury, the matter was officially closed.

Two documents were added to my permanent personnel file. One was a letter of commendation from the chief's office and a certificate naming me Officer of the Month for my actions taken during the robbery.

The other was a letter of reprimand from the chief's office for using a racial slur during contact with a citizen.

Thirty-Six

I was in the detective division offices after the killing at the chicken place. It was evening now, and I was tired. I had given my statements and done my reports. The case was a homicide, and would be handled with the depth and care given any other case in which one person killed another. I was ready to go home.

The chief called my friend Johnny at home and asked him to join me at the station. The chief knew there was no one at my home, so he told Johnny to go home with me, break out a bottle, and get drunk . . . sort of "get it out of my system." Johnny was my friend, so he agreed.

Problem was, I was as cold as ice inside. I felt an absolute stillness, and a bottle of very good whiskey had no effect on me . . . none. Johnny and I sat up until almost midnight. We drank, and I told him in magically clear detail of how I had killed that afternoon. We drank, and he listened, and I sat under the kitchen light with him and wondered about life and death and why and who and how.

My cold emotions absorbed the whiskey . . . Johnny got drunk. He got so drunk I was afraid to let him drive. I loaded him into my car and took him home to his wife. She gave me a hug and I drove off into the night.

Another good friend of mine, Russ, was working that night on the midnight shift. He was on the east side of town, near the beach. I drove around until I found him, then I sat on the hood of his car and shared coffee with him. He didn't ask too many questions or try to give advice. The inner being that was me recognized the questions that I would be asking for the rest of my life, but the emotional me sat becalmed.

When the sun came up I went home.

Thirty-Seven

I WAS lying on the floor beside a couch in the living room, with my service revolver drawn and pointed at the bedroom door. Two police officers senior to me, Ed "Brown Shirts Stop Bullets" and Mike "Mr. Glasses," stood on either side of the door with guns drawn.

Inside the bedroom was a black guy who had wounded his wife with a small handgun and then had locked himself in the bedroom of their duplex, firing an occasional round out of the window when it pleased him. We were able to get the wife out and she was on her way to the hospital. Now it was time for the guy with the gun.

Ed "Brown Shirts Stop Bullets" got his nickname because of his attitude. He could not be hurt. He was an ex-marine, he worked out with weights, he practiced at the firing range, he jogged for miles. He was tough. His muscles bulged, and his brown uniform shirt stretched tightly over his chest. He handled his calls aggressively, and if a physical confrontation arose he threw himself into it bodily, with great enthusiasm and élan.

Mike "Mr. Glasses" got his nickname from the black people in the area he worked. He was very big and wore glasses, and they called him sir and identified him to each other as "Mr. Glasses." It was probably better it had turned out that way. If it had been left to us to pick his nickname it surely would have been different. Did I say he was big? How about six-five and three hundred and some pounds? In briefing he literally pulled up a couple of chairs and sat down. He was huge . . . you should have seen what I looked like standing next to him. Comical.

So. The black guy refused to come out. We yelled at him and told him all the things we were supposed to tell him, but he just said, "No way," and that was that. This was before the days of SWAT and hostage negotiation and all that. This type of situation was handled on the squad level.

I watched wide-eyed as Ed and Mike nodded to each other grimly, their revolvers held firmly, barrels pointed up toward the ceiling. They were going in.

This was it.

Ed stepped back, tensed, and gave the bedroom door a mighty kick. It flew inward with a crash. At the same time he launched himself forward, gun hand outstretched. Simultaneously Mike hurled his bulk into the doorway, gun forward.

Oooff! Grunt! Uuunh!

"Brown Shirts Stop Bullets" and "Mr. Glasses" were jammed together in the doorway like a couple of cartoon characters, their hips locked, their feet kicking wildly. The harder they pushed against each other, squirming and wiggling, the firmer they became wedged in the doorway.

The black guy took one look at the two arms waving guns around the room, threw *his* gun out the window, and dove under the bed.

Finally after one last crushing heave Ed and Mike exploded into the room, falling all over each other and cursing loudly. They untangled themselves, looked around the room quickly, saw nothing but the open window, and looked at each other in confusion. "Brown Shirts Stop Bullets" yelled, "Bastard must've gone out the window . . . I'll bet they've got him outside!" and they turned and thundered past me and out the front door.

I stood there slightly dazed as the black guy crawled out from under the bed. He looked around nervously, then turned to me and mumbled sheepishly, "Man, I've been arrested before, but this is the first time I've ever seen anything like *that*."

Me and him both.

Thirty-Eight

I HAD been shot at.

I had been stabbed, and cut. I had been hit with a brick, a board, a bottle, and a car. I had been beaten and bitten. I had been choked and kicked, and had both thumbs dislocated on separate occasions.

I had been hospitalized with a concussion after the back of my head tried to duke it out with the hot asphalt of the street. I had been treated for an ulcer at age twenty-six, after four years on the job. I knew all about the emergency room, shots, stitches, butterfly bandages, and nurses.

This time was slightly different, and my wife was not pleased.

My right fist, at a high rate of speed and accuracy, and with a pleasing quickness and intensity, impacted the front teeth of a person I was arresting... effectively enough to put his felonious ass in the emergency room for some patching up before booking. Trouble was, my second knuckle bore the brunt of the punch, and the skin over the knuckle exploded open in a bright red star. There was a lot of blood, which only angered me at the time.

It was a busy night in the ER and one of the nurses took a fast look at my knuckle, cleaned it, asked me if I was caught up on my shots, and slapped a butterfly bandage on it. I finished up the night and went home. My hand ached during the night, but I had felt that before, and ignored it. I couldn't ignore it the next day however. My hand was swelling fast, reddening, and becoming extremely sensitive. I managed to get my uniform on, drove to the station, sat through the briefing, got into my unit and headed back down to the ER. By the time I pulled into the breezeway my hand was as big as a softball and there was a thin red line running up my arm. Uh-oh.

I walked in and showed my hand to a nurse. She didn't say anything, just motioned for me to wait. A moment later a doctor came back with her. He grabbed my hand, looked at it and my arm, turned away, and said, "You're admitted." Then he walked away.

I can't be admitted, I protested, I'm on duty, my unit is out front, the whole shmear. He stopped, came back, looked at me sternly through his glasses, and said quietly, "How about gaseous gangrene? You can wait another day if you like, then you can decide whether to just lose your hand or your whole arm." Then he turned away again.

I was admitted.

The four days in the hospital pass slowly. I am restless and bored, and it seems to take forever for the medicine to show results. My wife is quietly disapproving of the whole situation.

"It's stupid."

"Because I'm hurt on the job? That's stupid?"

"It's stupid to punch someone in the mouth with your fist, it doesn't help in the arrest, and it only proves you're not as tough as you think you are."

"Huh?"

'The dirtiest place on this planet is in someone else's mouth. Punching someone in the teeth is a guaranteed way of getting infected, as you have so unwittingly displayed."

What if I had been shot?"

"It's stupid."

"What if I had been run over again, or stabbed again, or hit with a bottle again? Would that be better?"

"Still stupid, it's just stupid."

"Jesus, honey, getting hurt is one of the things that sometimes happen with this job, you know that."

"I know that other cops go thirty years without firing their gun, without shooting and killing someone. Other cops don't get gangrene from punching people in the mouth, they don't get stabbed or run over either. They get promoted, assigned to inside jobs, jobs where they use their heads. I know that other cops belong to churches, become scout leaders, take up scuba diving, teach school... they *do* things, *different* things. They don't do the job, job, job... all the time and forever the job! And they don't use their bodies like some kind of macho sacrificial weapon to accomplish their mission!" She takes a deep breath and charges on. "There are other people out there doing *other things*, positive things with their lives. There is a whole world out there that doesn't even know what a 'hot sheet' or *APB* is... people are out there living *real* lives, in peace."

She bites her lip, close to tears. I sigh. We look into each other's eyes. "I didn't purposely go out to get hurt," I say quietly, "but it happens in *my* real world. Next time I'll try to get hurt in some acceptable way, all right?"

"It's still stupid. This life *we* live is stupid," she says, and walks out of the room.

Thirty-Nine

I WAS only a couple of blocks away when the call came down ... signal-four motorcycle, with injuries, three hundred block State Road 84. As I arrived and jumped out of my unit I could see a car stopped across the outer two lanes of the eastbound side of the roadway. There was an old man standing beside it, holding his head. Beside the car, lying on its side with the front end crumpled, was the motorcycle. Two bodies were on the pavement. One was surrounded by people bending over and holding towels. As I ran up I saw that it was a teenage boy, he was sitting up, and there was blood on his face. A man who was holding a towel to the boy's face looked up at me and said tensely, "This one's got glass in his face. We need an ambulance. I don't think there's anything you can do for the other one."

That was why there was a crowd around the one kid and no one near the other. They thought the other one was dead.

I confirmed with the dispatcher that EMS was on the way as I ran over to the other kid. He too was a teenager, thin build, medium-long hair. He lay flat on his back, arms stretched out at his sides, hands balled into fists. His helmet was off and lying a few feet from his head. He stared straight up into the clear sky with half-open eyes, and he did not move. I could see no head injuries, but there was a lot of blood under his jaw, and covering his chest. His chest did not move.

I lifted one eyelid, looked into his eye, and said, "Hey. Can you hear me? Are you in there?"

Nothing.

His eyes had that look, you know, that half-open cloudy staring look that says, Goodbye.

I knelt over him, cocked his head back, opened his mouth, placed mine over his, and blew. There was a lot of burbling and blood spattered my face, but the chest did not move. I blew again. The same thing, but this time he hiccupped.

Could be nerve action. Could be my own air backing up. Could be he was still alive.

I looked up and saw a guy standing there watching intently. I yelled at him, "My trunk's open . . . bring me the heavy green metal box, it's oxygen!" The guy ran off and I breathed again into the kid's mouth. That time I thought I saw the chest move slightly, but not enough, and there was still that loud burbling and blood spattered everywhere. I didn't even look up when I heard the oxygen hit the pavement by my leg. The guy already had it open and I reached in and grabbed the valve tool and the face mask and got it hooked up and slammed it onto the kid's face and opened the valve. I had it on the open setting; it would pump a continuous stream of oxygen into the kid's mouth.

There was a horrible rubbery-wet slobbering noise, blood and body fluids blew up all over my hand and wrist, and the chest did not move.

I kept the mask on the kid and leaned closer and looked down at his throat. Shit. This had been the driver of the motorcycle. When the bike impacted the car this kid had been rocketed forward and upward. He had hit the car along the upper part of the driver's window with his throat. His throat was crushed, pulped, and ripped open. I looked down at the bloody mass of tissue and watched as the oxygen I was pumping into the mouth escaped from a jagged hole in the throat.

I covered the throat with the flat of my hand and tried to block the hole. Instead of his chest rising as I had hoped, the oxygen backed up, the kid's cheeks puffed out, and the mask slid off his face.

God*dammit.*

I looked at the kid's half-open eyes and watched as his body convulsed on the hard pavement. The damn kid was gonna die right there while I watched. No. No, no, no. His eyes closed tight, he arched his head back, his neck muscles straining, and he gulped hard twice. Then he was still.

No.

I pulled my hand off his throat and looked closer. There was so much damage that when I put the flat of my hand down it just pushed the whole mess onto and into the airway, blocking it completely. I dropped the oxygen mask and ripped into his throat with my hands. With my fingers I dug into the blood and mess and tore open the skin. His skin was wet and slippery and tough, and I had to dig and pull very hard to make any progress. Finally I could see the interior of the throat clearly, the reinforced tube that is the airway was right there. I spread it back as best I could, clamped the mask right over the throat, and covered the kid's mouth with one bloody hand.

The oxygen crashed into the airway and impacted the kid's chest. It moved. I could see it move and I said through clenched teeth, "Come on ... come on ... come *on!*" The chest heaved, and then again, and I felt first vomit and then belched air between my fingers. "Come *on!*" The chest heaved, the kid's eyes closed, he turned his head, and gagged. "All right! C'mon, kid ... come on!"

I heard a crash and looked up to see the guy who had brought my oxygen. He had gone back for my first aid kit, and in his hurry had dropped the metal box by my side. I nodded at him and told him to grab one of the big compresses from the box. He fumbled with the box and I concentrated on keeping the face mask on the kid's throat. The mask was designed for a face, not a throat, and I wasn't getting a good seal. There was still too much oxygen escaping, blood and mess blowing all over the pavement, the kid's chest, and my arms. The guy nudged me and I took the compress from him, already open. In one motion I removed the mask from the throat, pushed back all the ripped skin, and covered the whole area gently with the compress. Then I cocked the kid's head back again, opened the mouth, and fit the mask over his face. I reached over and changed the setting to Resuscitate. This would force the oxygen into the kid's chest in such a way that the body would begin to breathe normally. Maybe.

I had a good seal on everything now, and watched and listened as the oxygen flowed, then stopped, flowed, then stopped. The kid's eyes closed and I saw his body relax, first the neck muscles, then the arms, and finally the fists. His hands opened flat against the street. The chest rose and fell, rose and fell.

"All *right!*"

A few seconds later came more sirens, doors slamming, guys running. Two medics knelt beside me, watching. I looked into their intense faces and said, "Crushed throat. No oxygen, or very little, for a couple of minutes." They nodded and went to work. I kept the oxygen going while they did their thing, and finally one said, "We got it," and my mask was pulled off to be replaced by theirs. Then the kid was on the stretcher and in the back of the ambulance and gone. I looked over my shoulder and saw that the other kid was already gone too, and that traffic guys were there working the accident scene. I saw that the crowd had been pushed back to the sidewalk and things were under control. I looked around for the guy that had brought my equipment but he was gone. I never learned his name or thanked him.

As I knelt on that hot pavement and looked down at my bloody hands and arms I didn't know that a short while later I would be standing in the emergency room and the kid's mother would be introduced to me by my lieutenant. I didn't know that she would be told by the medics and emergency room doctor that I had saved her son's life. I didn't know that she would stand in front of me, still in shock, squeezing my hand and trying to say "Thank you." I didn't know that the kid would live, but he would, and within what seemed like an incredibly short time he recovered completely, with full use of his throat and voice.

I didn't know any of it. I could only know that I had ripped
into his throat with my bare hands, and had torn his flesh with
my fingers. I could only kneel there on that blacktop altar, and
look down at the offering of blood on my palms, and guess at
the coming judgment.

Forty

I HAD been exiled to the Communications Center again. I lan-
guished there for a couple of months, waiting impatiently to be
reassigned to the street. For me, being taken away from the
street was cruel punishment, and maybe the brass knew it,
because that's what they would do to me every time I got into
trouble. My last incident involved what was termed "excessive
use of force" and "falsifying a police report"—meaning I had
beat some dirtbag's ass and disputed his version of it in my
report. The dirtbag's parents complained to the department,
and rather than get into a protracted and costly investigation
to find the total truth, the easy way was taken. The dirtbag's
parents were mollified by my transfer off the street and other
"severe disciplinary actions." No lawsuit, no investigation, no
truth.

I was going through the motions, biding my time, and I began
to notice some things about myself that worried me. I admitted
to myself that these worrisome things had been with me for
some time now and I had been ignoring them, but recently
they had festered and inflamed like a wild emotional acne. My
wife and I were beyond being ships passing in the night... at
least they displayed recognition lights... and I was becoming

more withdrawn, even from those I worked with and counted on.

I asked to see the comm sergeant, and told him I thought I needed help. To his credit he immediately referred me to the chief's office. After sitting in the outer office feeling numb for a few minutes I was ushered in to the chief's presence. I told him I thought I needed help. To his credit, he listened, and he took action.

This was in the days before psychological testing before hiring, or ongoing counseling on the job. There was very little precedent regarding the funding of this type of program. We're talking just plain money here, and we all know how sensitive municipal administrations can be about that. I argued, and to his credit the chief argued, that if I broke my wrist on the job I would be treated for it at the proper medical facility, and the cost would be covered by the city. In this case I was mentally and emotionally injured as a direct result of my job, and the help I needed should be funded by the city. To their credit, the city agreed with the chief, and I was given a series of appointments with a psychiatrist.

The doctor was a kindly, caring, and knowledgeable gentleman who gave me the basic tests, asked me subtle and non-threatening questions about myself, and listened to my own diagnosis. Then he wrote a letter to the chief.

See, the chief had promised to help me, but only if I would agree with the doctor's final evaluation and recommendation. If the doctor thought I could be a cop, then I would keep my job. If not, the chief could only keep me on under the onus of "negligent retention," which would make him vulnerable to potential future lawsuits.

The doctor's letter was six pages long, and everyone who read it agreed it was a masterpiece of ambiguity. There was some question that I *should* be a cop, he said, but there was no question that I *could* be a cop. I could do the work, but I probably wasn't cut out for it. The chief, to his credit, looked at me, shrugged his shoulders, and told me he would take the chance. I could keep my job, but if I screwed up again the letter could be interpreted in another way, and I would "be gone." I shook his hand and shuffled out, curiously unrelieved.

In retrospect I feel I had already bottomed out and was on my own self-motivated way up and out of the emotional black hole I had been in. Recognition of the problem is the first step, and I had recognized it and acknowledged it. I don't regret going through the counseling though... it was the beginning of a long overdue process of nurturing a positive relationship with myself.

One of the things the doctor told me on my last visit, when I asked him flat out if I should be a cop, was that he understood that I could be an effective police officer, but that I would pay a terrible price... he saw me as an artist, maybe a writer.

One of the good things that came from the experience was in the letter itself. From that time on if anyone accused me of being crazy, all I had to say was, "I'm not crazy... and I've got a six-page letter to prove it."

Forty-One

YOU GONNA hide?

You gonna run and hide *now?*

Man, you and your frien'-boy been skulkin' around that house so late at night. You and your bad man there tryin' to force open that front window and climb into that house with your sweaty gloves on and that nasty bit of rope in your pocket and that bad little gun in your hand?

But why you runnin' now, bad boy? Huh? Why you runnin' from us? You weren't gonna run from them two old people in that house, were you, my man? No... you goin' to be the *bad* motherfucker when you git into that man's house, uh-huh. Yeah, you and your partner gon' just be terrorizin' those folks all through the night, and then you be takin' everything they got when you be done.

But what happened, my man? Why, you looked over your bad shoulder and you done seen a couple of hard fuckin' poleeses creepin' up on your ass, huh? Yeah, here they come, and uh-oh...now you don't wanna be bad, now you wanna run. Yeah, *run*.

You mean you just turned and *split*, man? Just left your partner squatting there with big wide eyes and his mouth open as the hard poleeses don' come *crashin'* down on his head? Your bad legs was justa *carryin'* you around the corner and into the back yards as you heard the first sounds of those poleeses comin' *down* on your bad little frien'-boy, huh? And my, *my*, as you be runnin' through those back yards and over those fences and between those raggedy-assed bushes you just be *shuckin'* that rope and those gloves, and most certainly and for *sure* you be throwin' that little gun up onto a roof because even though you so bad it be unbelievable, you still don' wanna be caught by those hard poleeses with that gun in your hand, huh? Cause you know, don' you? You *know* those hard poleeses go to sleep at night hopin' and prayin' and dreamin' of the time they can be lucky enough to catch you bein' so bad with your gun in your hand. They *want* to catch you with it, bad boy, cause when they do they gonna blow your ass *away*. That right, *ain't it?*

So now you gonna hide? No, man...no.

Cause, guess what...what be trotting around the side of the house and into those back yards? Guess what be shoulderin' through those raggedy-assed bushes, stoppin' where you threw your gloves, and where you threw the rope? Yeah man, the poleeses are behind it, runnin' hard, comin' *on*. But guess what's leading the way? Guess what ain't never *heard* of Miranda, never *heard* of search and seizure? Guess what's with those hard poleeses, my man, that knows you stink, that knows your smelly fear leaves a trail, knows you be hidin' right there, *scared?*

You gonna hide now, man? You gonna hide and then be bad with the poleeses? No, man.

Cause you be layin' there in the dark, squirmed under that hedge, knowin' that the poleeses will walk right by you, and guess what? Here he *comes*, bad boy! That's right, one hundred and six pounds of totally, genuinely, purely *bad* German shepherd poleese dog... black and pink lips curled back, heavy tongue dripping saliva, unfuckingbelievable white razor teeth snapping, big paws digging in, chest heaving, ears flat back against his big square skull.

And he wants *you*.

He been followin' you, man, been followin' your filthy trail through all the yards. He been on your ass, and now he has arrived. Hey, my bad man... he don' know *nothin'* about your rights, you know? I mean, he just don' *know* about how we is all supposed to be treatin' you fairly, you know, treatin' you like you was a real part of society... treatin' you like you had some *rights* like those lawyers done be sayin' all the time. Even if somehow you could do some squirmin' and cryin' and shufflin' along on TV with your poor o-pressed head down and your sufferin' little lips poutin' and some sweet-dignity-of-man protectin' lawyer be standin' right there in that hedge right now, briefcase and all... guess what? He be takin' one look at what be comin' through that hedge at you, my man, and he be takin' all his writs and his motions-to-show-cause and his pin-striped suit, and he be makin' himself be *gone*. That's right, sucker... you bad, you *so* bad, and now you're alone and that poleese dog is *on you*.

Go ahead, *scream*, motherfucker! Throw up one sweaty arm and try to wriggle backwards in the dirt. It don' do no good, man. Kick your feet, go ahead, bad boy, kick your feet and roll around and scream and yell and cry. You ain't *bad*... you ain't *shit!* And that poleese dog been waitin' all night in the back of a car just to find you... find you and *eat you, motherfucker!*

You gonna hide?

No, man.

No.

Forty-Two

I HATE burglars.

There are crimes and there are crimes, and in my heart of hearts I think the most hideous is rape. But as far as the basic everyday crimes-against-the-people-living-in-my-zone thing goes, burglary really bothered me. I was put out there in my patrol unit to watch over things and then you'd call me during the shift and show me through your small business, or worse, your home. You'd show me where the burglar had cut the screen and broken the window, where he had ripped through your office or your bedroom. You'd tell me about what he took, and it used to hurt me. I would feel a burning in my guts, and intense pain, because you had been violated.

Residential burglars bothered me the most because they forced their slimy way into your sanctum while you were out working to pay for the things you had. Residential burglars walk through your kitchen, rifle through your underwear, scatter your family pictures all over the place, and take those things that mean a great deal to you. Their greasy evil presence lingers behind, shattering the harmony of your castle.

In the south end we had some young residential burglars that were really staying busy for a while. Teenagers mostly, in their last year of high school if they were still there. Street dudes, smart, wiseass, and hard. The south end was my old neighborhood and I knew some of the families involved, and they knew me, or of me. When I began working day shift there

I wanted them all. I wanted to catch them inside a house, in the *act*.

With a little homework I eventually compiled a nice list of suspects. Any time I saw one of these lovelies I would check them out, pat them down, see what they had to say. I just liked to stay right on them so they knew that Officer Friendly really cared.

During one shift the area was getting clobbered with house burglaries and the word on the street put the blue finger on two different guys. They knew each other and hung out with the same crowd, but they didn't work together. One guy had real blond hair and a baby face, and he liked to work with a kid that was seventeen but looked around eleven. The other guy had a French name and long brown hair and the beginnings of a mustache. I was taking several B&E reports a week, standing there in the bedroom with my feet in all the underwear, looking at the dresser drawers dumped all over the place and hearing you tell me that your grandfather's opal ring really wasn't worth that much but it meant a lot to you.

I have always believed in the direct approach. I was the cop, and they were the burglars, and we needed to get that right on the line. So when I ran into both of these suspects on the street I patted them down and identified myself. I began easily enough, explaining about the high rate of B&E's in the neighborhood and admitting I was concerned about it. Then I got into their faces and told them I was sure they were the scumbags I was looking for, and that I prayed I would catch them in the act. I told them I had wonderful dreams about catching them *inside* and *in progress* so I could kick their ass. That was the message. I was out there looking, and I would find them if they kept it up. They could stop being burglars or they could move to Wyoming, but if they stayed with it I would find them, and when I did I was going to kick their motherfucking slimy piece of shit scumbag dirtball faces in.

It was a beautiful bright sunny day, clear and hot. I was cruising when a B&E in-progress call came in. The location was near me. An elderly woman was on the line advising she saw two young guys break a panel out of the back door of her neighbor's house. She was sure they were inside. I headed that way and heard one of the juvenile units come on and say he was close also. He would take the front and I would take the rear.

I rolled the car in neutral down the street, eased to a stop, opened the door quietly, and went running across the yards, feeling the adrenalin and anticipation. I came in a crouch through the bushes and saw the back door standing open. Moved closer and could hear pounding and crashing inside... and laughter.

I eased up beside the rear door and saw that it entered into a small utility room and then the kitchen. Stood there with my gun in my hand, waiting.

When the juvenile officer pulled his car up in front of the house the laughter stopped. There was heated whispering for a few seconds, and then here they came. It was the blond-haired baby-faced kid and his little partner. One had a camera and the other a jewelry box. They came running through the kitchen and slid to a stop in the utility room, both staring wide-eyed at the barrel of my .38.

Hello, scumbags.

I put them both in the spread position against the washer and dryer. The little one began snuffling and whimpering and I told him to save it for the judge. The other one began to say something and I reminded him of the conversation we had had a couple of days ago. He started to push away from the position and swing around, and when he did I came off the balls of my feet and kicked him as hard as I could right between the legs. I kicked him so hard he actually lifted into the air a couple of feet before falling to the floor. I kicked him so hard that if there had been an NFL scout there I would have been working only on Sundays from then on. It was one of the most beautiful, perfectly placed, effective kicks I have ever made. It was a classic. The kid let out a scream and fell in a huddle to the floor.

Later we had to carry him to the juvenile unit to be taken in and booked. He and his little partner were eventually sent off to one of the programs and I hardly ever saw him again. Maybe he's still a burglar, or a parole officer, or a member of the Vienna Boys' Choir. Whatever.

I like to think he'll remember that kick for the rest of his life.

Evening shift came around and we had another problem. Someone was breaking into the middle school down by the Little League stadium and trashing it. I mean, they stole stuff—radios, teaching aids, microscopes, typewriters, stuff like that ... but mostly they would just vandalize the rooms and the offices and equipment. I took a report once in the science department in a chemistry room. Everything had been smashed, all the beakers and tubes and burners and tools. Chemicals were scattered, the word FUCK was scrawled on the blackboard, and there was a large pile of human excrement on the teacher's desk.

Swell.

A couple of days later I slid up to the front of the school to check it out. It was early evening, about six. I jumped the chain link fence and began wandering the halls. Everything seemed quiet at first, and then I began hearing pounding and other noises. I moved faster toward the south end of the school, and got to the point where I could clearly hear a couple of guys laughing and carrying on and smashing things. I eased my head around a corner and there they were. One was the kid with the French name, and the other was his half brother. The glass was smashed out of the door to the shop and several of the lockers were ripped open. There were books and papers and notebooks and sweaters and flutes and lunchboxes and radios and sneakers and drumsticks and gym uniforms and makeup kits and photographs scattered all over the hallway. The two guys were busy ripping open more lockers and rummaging through them.

I stepped from the shadows and began walking at a steady pace toward them. I got about twenty feet away before the half-brother looked up and saw me. He didn't say anything, he just turned and bolted down the hallway. The kid with the French name didn't see me, but he saw his partner turn and run. Then he stopped, looked around, and there I was. He turned and ran.

I chased them both through the now nearly dark hallways. The half-brother made it around a corner and up onto a fence, then he was over it and gone. The kid with the French name made the corner and then I was on him. Our momentum carried us forward and we crashed into a wall. We were in an alcove formed by the hallway and the blocking fence.

Now, sucker.

I grabbed him by the hair and screamed into his ear, "It's *me*, man! It's me... and now I'm gonna *kill* you, asshole!" I didn't use restraining holds or try to "subdue" the suspect. I didn't put him into the "position." I just beat the piss out of him. I smashed him from one wall to the other. I punched him and kicked him and threw him. His face went bloody and I crashed it into first one side of the hallway and then the other, smearing the walls. Finally he went down, and I stood over him with my fists clenched, hissing the air out between my teeth.

A complaint by the burglar's family triggered an internal police investigation. These are fairly common, and most police departments try vigorously and aggressively to determine what really happened, to see if their officer went too far. Our Internal Affairs unit was, like most, directly tied to the chief's office, and was staffed by veteran, experienced, and loyal cops. People who push for "civilian review boards" to look into such matters don't want to hear it, but the police can and *do* police themselves. A cop knows another cop better than most non-cops, knows how he thinks, has had similar experiences, maybe in the past he has felt the fear, smelled the charged ozone of an insane night, tasted blood. Any chief, being an administrator first and a cop last, must look to the good of the whole against the fairness to the one. He and his loyal staff seek the truth, yes, but if there are layers of truth, he will usually recognize only that one that will do the least damage to his department and his city. Often this means that what the cop sees as truth is ignored. It is common for municipalities to settle out of court with a plaintiff's family rather than battle it out in front of a judge. It is cheaper. There are often minimum amounts of settlement, say ten thousand dollars, that a city attorney will offer a plaintiff at just the first glance at a case that might require some effort to prove the cop was correct in his actions. What the officer feels about this is pushed aside for the greater good. If the internal investigation showed enough evidence that the officer acted improperly, then the case would be passed on to the state attorney's office to be reviewed for criminal charges against the officer.

In my case with the burglar, it went to the state attorney, but after *that* investigation I was not charged. Then it's over, right? Wrong. Then it goes back to the department, and a review board that might say, Sure, Cherokee, you were not criminally charged in this incident, but we find that you broke several *departmental* rules. The punishment might be a transfer to another, less visible assignment. I might be "passed over" for promotion, or maybe I would be suspended without pay for a day, three days, five, a couple of weeks.

Besides professional sports, can you tell me of another job where you can be found innocent of breaking any laws and stilled be *fined*, still have your wages taken out of your pocket? Double jeopardy? I'm told there isn't.

I was suspended without pay a couple of times during my tenure with the Fort Lauderdale Police Department. Once, for three weeks, I took a demolition job with a construction firm to keep a paycheck coming in (I actually took home more money during this time than I would have as a cop). Yes, a policeman's lot is not a happy one, and certainly the police must be policed, but I thought we learned in Vietnam about going to war half-way. All the old sour-grapes sayings like "You send the cops out to do a tough job, but you handcuff them first" spring to mind, but I won't repeat them here. I will say, though, that I have respect for the new and younger generation of cop, and I think in many ways he or she is smarter than I was. Many of them carry their own insurance policies, medical *and* liability, and some of them even retain their own lawyers on a full-time basis. What I'm describing doesn't only apply to Fort Lauderdale, of course. It is the same with police departments all over the country, with NYPD and LAPD and many smaller ones in between.

Police officers' attitudes and actions are a reflection of our society's needs and weaknesses. Many times I willingly walked into the deadly arena that is the street, heard the door slam behind me, and sensed you were turning your backs, in righteous indignation, on me—and on yourselves.

Think what you like. As far as I'm concerned, all that blood splattered on those hallway walls looked a lot better than that pile of shit on the chemistry teacher's desk.

Forty-Three

WE ROLLED code three on a statistic.

The nine-year-old had gone next door to the eight-year-old's house to play. The eight-year-old proudly showed his friend his dad's high-caliber hunting rifle, which had been standing behind the door in the bedroom. They took it out into the back yard to play, excited and happy. The nine-year-old turned to say something to the eight year old, who held the rifle waist high. The roar of the rifle going off could be heard for blocks.

When we arrived and ran into the back yard we found the nine-year-old sitting on the ground, the eight-year-old still held the hot-barrelled rifle, his face ashen. The bullet had exploded into the nine-year-old's stomach, causing most of his intestines to be blown back out the entry wound. The nine-year-old sat there holding his insides in both hands, crying. As I knelt beside him and placed my hands on his shoulders to lay him down he said to me quietly, "I don't want to die... can you put me back together?" The eight-year-old, who at that moment began a lifelong emotional journey through a world from a Salvador Dali painting, looked at his friend and then down at the rifle in clear and irrevocable understanding.

The nine-year-old died, and the emotionally devastating ripple effect of what happened to him, and how, shattered the entire circle of two families.

We rolled code three on a statistic.

The six-year-old girl and her twin brother played in the bedroom while the babysitter prepared their lunch. The girl opened the night-table drawer and found the .357 Magnum revolver kept there in the event some scumbag from the street tried to come into the house some night and violate mommy and take daddy's cameras. The twin brother watched curiously as the six-year-old girl held the gun in both hands, pulled back the trigger, and...

Enough.

Believe me, I'm conversant with and comprehending of all the arguments for private ownership of weapons in this country. I've been around weapons all of my life, and I've used them for their designed purposes. I know all about the sporting life, but when I need meat for my table now I drive to the closest grocery store and buy it in convenient packages. I know all about crime in the streets too, and know of the minute number of homicidal bad guys and rapists killed by home guns each year versus the slaughter of innocents.

Yeah, I know all about guns and the Constitution and ideals and freedom.

But god*damn*, the reality.

Forty-Four

THE GIRL was nineteen, pretty, and away from her boyfriend for the night. She was in a funny mood; lonely, but not wanting to be with people. She went to the movies.

The hunter was a twenty-three-year-old carnival worker with a full head of hair, a round face, huge muscular shoulders and arms, heavy rough hands, solid thick legs, and a small penis. He was in a predatory mood. He had worked hard all day setting up the carnival machinery, waiting. Now it was nighttime and he was off, free. He went hunting.

The girl came out of the theater, drifted away from the crowd walking through the parking lot, and walked up to her car. As she stopped to unlock the door she was grabbed from behind roughly and the hunter opened the car door with one hand and shoved her inside, pushing her across the seat but still holding onto her. Then he climbed in behind the wheel and turned to her. His big leather belt was wrapped around his right fist, with the heavy metal belt buckle tight against his knuckles. He grabbed the girl by the hair with his left hand, stuck the belt buckle against her face hard, and said, "You do what I say, baby... or I'll start smashin' your fuckin' face with this here and I won't stop 'til your face is pulp. Hear?"

The girl, terrified, managed to shake her head. Then she felt his huge hand pushing her down onto the floorboards on the passenger side of the car. She sat like that, weeping, while the hunter drove her car out of the lot and then up and down the side streets, stopping occasionally, but then moving on. When she tried to look up he hissed and thumped her on the head with the buckle. Finally the girl felt the car bumping on an uneven road and then slowing. When the car stopped she could hear machinery running and as the hunter let her sit up she could see bright lights a short way off, and what looked like stadium lights nearby.

The hunter grabbed the girl, pulled her to him, and began kissing her face and neck. The girl cried out and struggled against him so he grabbed her by the neck and pushed his fist with the belt buckle against her cheek and said, "Motherfuckin' cunt. Shut your mouth and don't be fightin' me or I swear I'll kill you . . ." He had his big face close to hers and his sweat fell on her. She looked into his screaming eyes and knew in her heart she could not fight him. She knew he would kill her or cripple her for life, and she was afraid.

He tore her top open and began licking her breasts and grabbing them with his rough hands. She put her head back and groaned, sobbing. He heard her and misunderstood and laughed. Then he reached one hand down into her pants and fumbled around, breathing heavily.

"Take off your clothes, baby . . . take 'em all off . . . I want to see you."

He crouched over her grinning as she struggled on the carseat, finally wriggling out of everything and lying back naked. He undid his pants and stared at her and reached in and began fondling himself, grinning at her and licking his lips. They stayed like that for a few seconds and then he growled and grabbed her by the hair again, backing out of the car and taking her with him. Then he spun her around, pulled his pants down around his knees, and sat on the front seat with his legs spread in front of him. He pulled her roughly down into the dirt and said, "Suck it."

She looked up at him, saw the huge fist with the buckle, saw the sweat on his face, felt the dirt on her legs, and put her face tentatively between his knees. He grabbed her by the back of the head and pulled her against his crotch.

"I said *suck it...*"

After a few minutes he pushed her away from him and she fell into the dirt. She lay there crying softly until he said, "Get up. Get up and dance for me. I want to see your titties bounce. Get up and dance for me." The girl looked at him, confused, and stayed in the dirt. He made a quick move toward her and barked, "I said dance for me, *cunt!*"

Crying, the girl jumped up and stood there awkwardly. Big tears ran down her face and her hands hung limp at her sides. She was totally ashamed, hurt, and scared... and very close to not caring anymore. He hissed and moved again and she looked at him and started moving her body slowly, her feet in the dirt, the sound of machinery in her ears, bright lights nearby, and a cold forever wound in her heart.

He sat there with his legs spread, laughing softly and playing with himself. He masturbated slowly at first, but as he watched the girl he moved faster and harder until he was breathing very heavily and had his huge head back. Suddenly he stopped, glared at the girl, and rasped, "Come here!" She stepped closer to him and he flicked one arm out, caught her, and dragged her to her knees in front of him. He held her tightly by the hair, grinned at her, pulled her close, and ejaculated on her face. He held her like that as he finished. Then, gulping for air, he pushed her away and she fell into the dirt and lay there crying.

In a few minutes he grabbed her again and forced her back into the car. He climbed in beside her, started the car, and began to drive slowly. "Get back down on the floor, and put your clothes on." he said gently. As the girl struggled into her slacks she felt the car moving and heard the sound of machinery fading. She wiped her face with her top, and then put it on. Then she huddled on the floor, sobbing quietly.

A few minutes later she felt the car stop and looked up to see the hunter smiling at her. He patted her on the head and said, "Thanks, baby." Then he was gone. She stayed wrapped around herself, crying.

* * *

Scott was cruising slowly through the parking lot in his marked unit when he saw the girl standing by her car, head hanging down. She did not look up as he drove by, and he could see that her clothes were torn and she looked dirty and unsteady. He stopped, backed up quickly, got out of his unit, and walked up to her. As he approached, the girl looked up fearfully, saw him, and threw herself into his arms, sobbing violently.

I was just clearing a call in the north end of the zone when the information came out on the radio. It was a rape, no long time delay, and it sounded legit. A supervisor and some detectives were on the way to the parking lot and Scott was putting out a description. The guy we wanted was a big dude with lots of hair, wearing some kind of green work pants and a blue pull-over. He would also have a wide leather belt with a heavy buckle. I headed south toward where the victim had been located.

The supervisor wanted to know where the crime had occurred for jurisdictional reasons. A few minutes went by and then Scott advised that the victim had heard machinery running, had seen bright lights, and had seen what appeared to be stadium lights.

I had grown up in the south end. I knew it very well, every nook and cranny. On my side of the Davie Bridge there were only two places with stadium lights. No problem, but it was after ten at night. Bright lights? Machinery running? I drove to the Croissant Park school grounds. There were softball fields there, and near it was a railroad freight terminal. Now it was quiet, no one using the ballfields, and no train activity.

I headed south on Fourth Avenue toward Little Yankee Stadium. It was just south of a middle school. I knew the stadium lights were there, but what about the bright lights and the machinery?

Scott came on the radio and asked that I switch over to the records channel so we could talk.

"You there, CP?"

"Yeah."

"This happened close to here, CP. This just went down, and I think this guy is still in the area."

"I'm lookin', Scott."

"This is a bad one, CP, know what I mean? This guy did a job here . . . we need to find him as soon as possible."

I thought of Scott in the paycheck line with his daughter standing awkwardly next to him with her fingers clutching his pantleg.

Before I could respond he said it again.

"This is a bad one, CP."

I crossed State Road 84, passed the armory, looked into the distance at the stadium lights, and smiled. There, on the east grounds of the middle school, was a collection of trucks and cars and big vans and odd machinery and crazy-looking equipment. Bright lights were on and generators were running and I had found myself a carnival that had just arrived that day.

Hello, motherfucker.

I pulled my unit onto the grass and got out. I knew he would be there. I knew he would be mine.

I advised the dispatcher of my location and she advised me that she would try to find a backup for me. I wasn't worried about it. I wanted this dude, and I would get him with or without a backup. There was no movement on the grounds, all the workers had apparently finished up and gone to bed. I shined the beam from my flashlight around at the trucks and vans and walked slowly between pieces of machinery.

I found him sleeping on some tarpaulins in the back of a semitrailer.

I just stood there a moment, shining my light on him as he slept. I had been a working cop long enough to have that secret place in my heart that would defy all legal and administrative and judicial logic and simply *tell me* when I had my man. The hunter could have been lying there naked, or with a shaved head, or in a pair of purple swim trunks, and I *still* would have known. It was him it was him it was *him*.

For the record, the hunter had crawled on top of the tarpaulins and fallen asleep still wearing the dirty blue pullover and green work pants. The leather belt with buckle was dangling from one of his hands. This was practically a gimme.

I stood there in the dark with his hulking form captured in the beam of my flashlight. My mind flashed over other rapes I had handled, the stunned looks on the victim's faces, the shame in their eyes, the wounds in their bodies and hearts. I thought of the times I had watched the tears fall slowly down the soft cheeks as the bruised lips haltingly let the horrible story escape. I thought of the ripped slender hands clutching at the torn edges of cotton dresses, of the bare dirty feet on the cold floor, of the blood and dirt and skin under delicately painted nails. I stood there, a man, a cop... a tempered weapon. I had been bloodied and I was hardened and I knew what justice was and I was going to kill this slimebag with my hands my feet my teeth my revolver my heart my badge. I *knew* the truth, I *knew* the pain. *This sonofabitch had to die... tonight... now!*

"Well, you see, Your Honor... I tried to question the suspect and he went for my gun and I was in fear of my life so I had to shoot him in the balls and in the mouth and in the head and I had to reload and shoot him in the knees and in the cock and in the heart again and again and again. But look at it this way, Your Honor... he'll never rape again..."

"Gosh, chief... I mean, I tried to pat him down and he came at me with that big nasty belt buckle and I had to kick him in the balls and then get him with a beautiful snapping front kick which broke his knee and as he started to go down I had to take him with the blade of my left hand across his motherfucking nose and of course it broke and as it did I had to get him two or three or five times in the ribs and then finally, chief, I had to rip his throat out with my hands and pull his sweaty skin off his skull and gouge his eyes out with my fingers. But chief, listen, is he still out there? *Is he still out there, chief?*"

My entire self was tightened like a steel spring, my whole being trembled like an animal just before he springs. My blood pounded and my heart beat and my fists clenched. I longed to move, to *jump*, to take him as I knew I should, and as I knew he needed to be taken. My chest heaved as I breathed the hard night air, searching the possibilities.

But no.

The system. The system...us...the society...it is us, we are it. The system will take care of him...I am only a cop, not a judge. I am not the executioner. We have the Law.

All the feelings, all the emotion that formed that molten rush through my system internalized, pulled back inside me, rested in my heart and soul. I stood there in my uniform with my badge, and I proceeded forward as a cop would proceed, as a professional, as a working soldier of our judicial system.

I shined the light into the hunter's eyes and pounded on the side of the trailer. Finally he groaned and stirred and slowly sat up and growled, "Who the fuck is that with the light? Put that light outta my eyes, man." I jumped up into the trailer and walked slowly toward him, flicking the beam of light once over my uniform. Then I shined it back in his face and said quietly, "I'm the police, man...it's my light." I stopped a few feet from him and began talking.

After listening for a moment to my professional, sincere, and caring logic he agreed it would be better for him in the long run if he voluntarily came with me to the station to talk a certain situation over. I clearly read him the Miranda warnings off the card we carried. He shook his big head and stood up, dropping the belt to the floor of the trailer as he did so. Then he began to pull off his shirt.

I straightened up and said, "No, my man...leave it on." I smiled and continued, "It's just the police station. You can wear what you've got there. And don't forget your belt...we don't want your pants to fall down." He hesitated, saw something in my eyes, and complied.

He was docile as I patted him down, and I stuffed him into the backseat of my unit. I stared at the hunter and saw my reflection in the back window, my face next to his, and I wondered at how the tin lining of my heart kept the molten ball of fire inside me from causing a fiery meltdown.

* * *

The hunter was with the detectives for less than an hour when he admitted "meeting" the girl in the parking lot. He insisted he had done nothing wrong, but the detectives were already convinced he was their guy so they prepared to put him in a lineup. I happened to be in the booking area when they brought him in, and seeing my face as a familiar one, the hunter stood beside me and said quietly, "I could not have done what they say, officer, and I can prove it. I can't . . . it don't . . . I can't make it hard. I even had a doctor check me once. I couldna' done this thing." I included the conversation in my report and of course later on the girl picked him out of a lineup and he was charged.

As it turned out the hunter was charged with more than one rape. Other jurisdictions heard about the arrest and began contacting our detectives. The various reports showed that in many cities in the state when the carnival was in town at least one rape occurred. The rapist, described as big, had a consistent problem with his victims. He had great difficulty becoming aroused, and made his victims do different things to help him. In the police community he was known as the limp-dicked rapist.

Frog-eyed Jeff was the defense attorney assigned to the hunter's case. Jeff was a new guy in the public defender's office at that time and was dying to make a name for himself. He wore thick glasses, and one eye looked south while the other stole furtive glances to the north. He was small, loud, and obnoxious. He did not care about the victim in the hunter's case, and he didn't care about the hunter either. He only cared about how it would affect his reputation around the legal community.

The prosecutor was also a young guy, but he had some experience behind him. He was like Jeff in his desire to make a name for himself, but was different in that he did care for the victim. He did his best, working within the rules of court procedure, to protect the victim from the terrible workings of the court.

It wasn't enough.

When Frog-eyed Jeff took the girl's deposition it totalled 110 pages.

"Have you seen your boyfriend's penis?"

"How long is your boyfriend's penis?"

"Do you like sex?"

"Did you know the defendant before the night in question?"

"Did you offer the defendant a ride?"

"Did you enjoy performing fellatio on the defendant?"

"Did you smile at the defendant? Did *he* take off your clothes, or did you?"

"Did you dance for the defendant... to arouse him?"

When the case finally went to court it lasted three full days. It was a jury trial, and Frog-eyed Jeff outdid himself trying to prove to the world he was a real live attorney.

During the trial the victim sat huddled and hurting ("Your Honor, I ask that the court admonish the prosecution witness and plaintiff not to sit in such a forlorn and beaten manner, which I suggest is contrived.... This will prejudice the jury..."), the hunter sat subdued and morose, and the police officers trooped in and out laying down all the necessary information for the court. The prosecutor would have the cop lay out his evidence in direct, and then Jeff would attack them and their evidence in cross-examination. He attacked me too, but it was a mistake. The jury liked me, and I had been around long enough to have my lines locked right into the rules. Of course in a rape trial the big evidence comes from the testimony of the victim, her identification of the rapist and so forth. For the girl, having to get on the stand during direct was agony even though she was being questioned by the prosecutor, who was trying to take it easy on her and still get the things he needed from her. It was terrible for her, but she hung in there and then it was Frog-eyed Jeff's turn.

The way the time worked out, the cross-examination would occur after the dinner break. This meant the courtroom would be empty, because the normal working day was over, and the spectators and what not would have gone home. Even in an almost empty courtroom it would have been a very difficult thing for the girl to sit through Jeff's questioning. Jeff knew this and he wanted to make it as hard as possible for her. He wanted to win the case real bad.

So Jeff got busy in the public defender's office. He went around to all his pals and the young secretaries and anyone who would listen, and using whatever arguments he had to, talked a large number of people into coming to the courtroom as spectators that evening. Most of them were in their early to middle twenties, guys and girls, singles and couples. They were interested professionally or they thought they could learn something or they were just curious.

When the girl was called to take the stand that evening for cross-examination she looked out into a courtroom filled with young people. Jeff's questioning of the girl went on for over two hours.

Three times she ran from the room, crying.

"So tell us, tell the court if you please. Isn't it true you smiled at the defendant and invited him to go for a ride?"

"Isn't it true you have previously testified that you like to perform fellatio on your boyfriend?"

She sat there on that lonely stand and her head was filled with the roaring of machinery and the flash of lights and the feel of cold dirt on her wet skin. She sat there feeling dirty while she looked out on a room full of clean innocent people.

"Isn't it true you have previously testified that you like sex, that you lost your virginity 'a couple of years ago'?"

"Did you tell the court that the defendant ejaculated? How do you know he ejaculated? Where did he ejaculate?"

The roar of the machinery muffled the sound of the lawyer's harping questions and she could hear her hair brushing against the muscular leg, could hear the skin slapping as he touched himself. Her senses were filled with the smell of him, of her, of the wet night. She felt the dirt on the witness-stand chair, and she felt dirty.

"Did you resist? Isn't it true that *you* took your clothes off?

Isn't it true you danced for the defendant, to arouse him? Isn't it true isn't it true isn't it true?"

She sat surrounded by staring eyes, clean eyes that mocked her filthiness and looked down at her slutiness and she huddled on the cold leather chair and felt the fear and the shame and the humiliation and the emptiness.

Three times she bolted from the stand and ran away.

Three times she went back ... and faced them all.

While the jury was out I made a promise that if the hunter was convicted I would come back when the sentence was finally handed down. The jury came back, and they found the hunter guilty guilty guilty.

To this day I believe the jury hated Frog-eyed Jeff so much by the end of the trial they would have found the hunter guilty no matter what had been said.

I went back for the sentencing weeks later, after the pre-sentencing investigation had been done for the judge. The judge looked down at the hunter standing before him in leg shackles and handcuffs and sentenced him to eighty-five years in jail. The hunter looked stunned and Frog-eyed Jeff looked bored and the young prosecutor looked vindicated and I looked around the room with my fists clenched and said, "*Yeah.*"

I made it a point to be in the hallway when they brought him out. I wanted him to see me there. I wanted him to know that I knew.

Goodbye, motherfucker.

I heard later that the girl moved from the area to try and start a new life for herself. I hope she no longer hears the roaring in her ears. Maybe she found peace.

The hunter carried that particular rape off to jail with him. He may even still be in there, but I doubt it. He may have found Jesus, or learned macramé, or written a book or something. He's probably paroled by now ... out hunting.

Jeff went on to become a successful defense attorney. But not for the public defender's officer, oh no. Now he's big-time, taking care of smugglers and other rich innocent types. He carried that particular rape all the way out into the hallway the night the jury found his client guilty.

Of course the girl, wherever she is, will carry that particular rape inside her for the rest of her life.

And so will I.

Forty-Five

"OH, YOU'RE here! I was afraid you wouldn't get my note... I had to sneak down there to the patrol office to leave it in your mailbox."

"Yeah. Well, I was thinking about coming out tonight... this just makes it better..."

"No problems on the home front about going out to this infamous cop bar without your wife?"

"Uh, no... she had to go to some school party, some professor of hers has these get-togethers, I guess."

"Sounds boring."

"Yeah."

"Want to hear something? I have a friend who's husband works for Palm Beach County S.O.... he told her the patrol guys up there know who you are, especially since that time you and Johnny chased that signal forty-one, signal-ten suspect up there and beat his butt after he ran into the side of that school..."

"Yeah? We must have made an impression..."

"*You* made an impression, that's for sure... and not only in Palm Beach..."

"Um...want another drink?"

"Sure. Hmmm, your palm feels warm...feels good. Do you mind if I hold your hand? Feels like my skin likes your skin..."

"No, I mean yes...I mean...yeah, you're right."

"Hey, I like it when you look at me like that. I um, I just had a thought...I wonder...if the skin of our *hands* feels so good touching, what would it feel like if..."

"I wonder too. Wanna go down to Hollywood Beach and look at the moon or somethin'?"

Forty-Six

IT WAS late at night, one of the quiet nights when phrases like "the sleeping city" feel right. John and I had eased our units up the circular ramp of the Burdine's parking garage until we reached the roof level. We were standing in the southwest corner of the top of the garage, and from there we could see off across the railroad tracks and out over the entire Himmarshee Village area of town. It was all old and rundown at that time, a haven for drifters and winos and other street types. From three stories up, on a clear night with the glow from the streetlights and occasional shop light, it was almost pretty. There was no train, no cars, hardly any movement at all...quiet, and peaceful.

We were standing there talking, you know, departmental gossip, dreams of fishing boats and hunting ducks, when we saw a movement and heard the distant scrape of shoes on pavement. We looked over the edge, down toward the street below. There, weaving in and out of the glow from the streetlights, listing first to one side and then the other, came one of the local winos known as Freddy.

Freddy was headed in a generally northern direction on the street just below us. He was a little loose, having trouble navigating the white line in the middle of the street, and the only firm thing about him was the grip on the paper-bag-wrapped wine bottle in his left hand.

John waited until Freddy was directly below us, his figure foreshortened by our height and muted by the shadows at the edge of the light. Freddy's round, almost bald head weaved back and forth as his eyes tried to follow the path of his feet. He stopped in his tracks as John, in a deep and booming voice, called, "*Freddy...*"

Freddy's arms waved around his sides, the wine bottle helping him maintain balance. John called again, "*Freddy! Freddy! Can you hear my voice, Freddy...?*"

Freddy stood there swaying, looking all around. He shook his head and tried to locate where the voice came from. The stillness of the night and the empty streets and the walls of the buildings helped give John's voice a strong, resonant quality, and it projected all over, bouncing here and there and echoing back occasionally. It sounded pretty impressive.

"*Freddy... I want you to look up! Look up into the night sky and look at me Freddy! It's the Lord, Freddy... the Lord is calling to you!*"

Freddy stiffened, his arms straight out at his sides. He put his head back, looked up into the night, almost fell over backwards, and croaked, "Jesus... I mean, hello Lord..."

John looked at me and smiled his patented angelic smile. Then he carried on, "*Freddy! This is the Lord... and I've been watching you lately. I'm not happy with what I've seen, do you understand, Freddy?*"

The little voice floated up to us, "Yes, Lord."

"*Let's face it, Freddy... you have been wasting the life I've given you. I am not pleased!*"

Freddy slid his left hand behind his back, wine bottle and

all. He looked up, squinted, and said, "Okay, Lord."

"Look, Freddy... I want you to make some changes for me, can you do that?"

"Sure thing, Lord."

"Good, Freddy! First I want you to get out of the middle of the street... go stand on the sidewalk!"

Freddy looked around, and keeping his left hand behind his back he circled around as he tried to back away from every direction over to the sidewalk. Then he looked up and shook his head.

"Good, Freddy! That was *very* good! Now, I want you to promise me you'll try to get yourself cleaned up in the morning, a *bath*, and some *clean clothes*! How about it?"

"No problem, Lord."

"Next, I want you to promise me that you'll try to find a job of some sort... maybe over at the Faith Farm, or the mission!"

Freddy brought out his wine bottle and almost took a sip, obviously feeling comfortable with the conversation to this point. Then he realized what he was doing and stuck it behind his back and looked all around him rapidly. He looked back into the night sky and croaked, "Sure thing, Lord, sure thing."

"And Freddy, I want you to promise me that you'll try to be nicer to all the other people I've put in this world! I like it when my people treat each other kindly!"

Freddy, feeling pretty smooth, grinned and said strongly, "You bet, Lord. I couldn't agree more... anything you say, Lord, anything at all."

John looked at me and smiled.

"*Anything*, Freddy?"

"Anything, Lord."

"Promise not to swear any more?"

"Yes, Lord."

"Promise not to be so lazy?"

"Yes, Lord."

"Promise to think of me once in a while?"

"Yes, Lord."

"Promise to throw that wine bottle you've got behind your back onto the street... smash it, get rid of it, and never *touch* a drop of wine again?"

Freddy brought the wine bottle around from his back. He held it with both hands, he fondled it, looked at it, and hugged it to his chest. He looked up with a straight back and in a firm voice he said evenly, "Go to hell, Lord... Sir!"

Then, as John and I tried not to let the sounds of our muffled laughter carry too far, Freddy walked off into the night, determination in his step and maybe a song in his heart.

It was refreshing to talk with someone who really knew what he wanted in this world.

Forty-Seven

SHE DIDN'T like her driver's license photo at all.

Less than a year ago she and some friends had gone together to take the test and after they passed everything they stood in line to get their picture taken and there was just one stupid little mirror and everyone was brushing their hair frantically and putting lipstick on so the picture wouldn't look *too* queer and then they waited in line and when it was her turn she moved her head when the camera operator said something and she wasn't ready when it went off and then she waited with her girlfriends for her name to be called. She grabbed her new license like the other girls and they walked out in a bunch, looking at each other's picture and giggling and rolling their eyes. She thought her hair looked nice and shiny, but thought her eyes looked tired and her lips looked too thin.

She kept her license in her small wallet and didn't show it to anyone.

I stood in the sun feeling the heat rise from the rough pavement of Seabreeze Boulevard. I stood at the edge of the roadway in the middle of the big curve that headed toward the beach off the causeway. I stood looking at her picture on her driver's license, thinking what a very pretty girl she was. The photo showed me one of those beautiful healthy California surfer-type girls, you know, with the long straight clean blonde hair and the glowing tanned face with perfect white teeth, full soft lips, a cute nose, and big lovely blue eyes. It was a picture of a teenage girl trying hard to be a woman, and I almost smiled, seeing the doubt in those young eyes staring at the camera.

I put the license in my pocket and walked toward her.

She lay on her back on the cruel hot street, her legs spread and her arms flung outward. Her hands were balled into loose delicate fists. She had been covered with an old army blanket by a guy who would later become a cop but who now just sat on the curb and stared at the sun. He had come along after it happened, and he covered her.

She had been riding on the back of her boyfriend's motorcycle wearing her jeans and a tube top and a helmet she hated because it made her face look too small. They had waited in the sun at the top of the Causeway Bridge, and when it finally closed and the gates went up they had come charging toward the beach, leading the pack. Her boyfriend could handle his bike, and he roared over the small bridge east of Pier 66 and then leaned it over nicely into the first curve on Seabreeze. The curve is not banked, and her boyfriend realized suddenly that speed and centrifugal force worked against them and he tried to slow down as they drifted toward the curb, and he almost made it. As her boyfriend leaned into the curve that same centrifugal force made her lean the other way, out, toward the curb and the sidewalk and the concrete light poles. The front tire of the motorcycle ripped into the unforgiving curb, the bike bounced once and went down, and her boyfriend was scraped and scratched up pretty good as he slid several feet on the rough asphalt.

At the same instant the bike went down, the right side of her face hit the brutal edge of a concrete light pole, her helmet shattered, and she cartwheeled off the bike. As her body slid on the asphalt her tube top was peeled down and when she finally stopped her breasts were exposed to the sun.

The guy who would later become a cop told me that was why he had covered her with his old army blanket. He had been a Beret in Vietnam and had seen blood, that didn't bother him. What bothered him was that her breasts were exposed and he was embarrassed for her because people were standing around and driving by slowly and they were all staring at her breasts. No one made any attempt to cover her . . . they just stared.

I took her license out of my pocket and looked at her face in the photo again, then I bent down and lifted the top corner of the army blanket. Some parts of her lower jaw were still there, and her left ear. Her left eye was still in the socket but it was impossible to tell what color it was. Where the skin was peeled back from her shattered facial bones and skull, it lay wet and bloody against her blonde hair, which was fanned out behind her.

The rest was gone. I looked into the open place that had been her face and tried mentally to reconstruct it. I could not. Her face was gone and the only tangible evidence we had that it ever existed was that awkward doubting nervous expectant sad little driver's license photo.

And she didn't like her driver's license photo at all.

Forty-Eight

THE RED light at northwest Seventh Avenue and Sixth Street has me waiting. I look over on the sidewalk and see him coming toward me. I wait to look at his face because it will lead to eye contact and then his bearing will change and I want to watch him being him for a few seconds.

His feet are pointed inward at an incredible angle, and they are covered in dirty gray sneakers. The outside edges of the sneakers are rubbed white from the constant scraping as he moves first one leg and then the other. I can't see if he's wearing socks because his pants are too long and bunched up at the cuff. The pants are some kind of double-knit checkered fabric, there is a small rip above one knee and dirty half-moons around each pocket.

He's wearing a gray sweatshirt that used to have some kind of logo or design on the front. Now there are just a few pieces of white and and orange paint sticking here and there across his chest. The arms coming out of the sleeves are thin, and the dull black skin is stretched tightly over knotted muscle. At the end of the thin arms his hands, with their long black fingers, flutter uncontrollably in front of him as he painfully walks toward me.

Finally I look at his face.

I can see he's not much older than me, but the face is screaming that he lives a thousand hard years every time he walks down the street. He has a square face with a good solid jaw. His ears look small, and lay flat against his skull. His hair is not long but unevenly cut, with wiry tufts sticking out here and there across the top of his head. As he gets closer I can see dust or lint or something clinging to the springy curls. His brow has a deep, dark, permanent crease from the scowl that is always there, the eyebrows knotted and bunched together. If there are times he is forced to laugh I know that brow releases the crease only fleetingly and reluctantly. His anger and frustration are signposted at that brow, working from there to his eyes, his nose, and finally his grim mouth.

Before he knows my eyes are on his I see him unguarded, or as unguarded as he ever allows himself to be in this world. As he awkwardly shuffles down the sidewalk his eyes are far away. He is looking down at the dirty concrete but he doesn't see it beneath his twisted feet. The deep burning pain, anger, frustration and confusion are perched at the surface, around the rims of those eyes which are cloudy and out of focus. Normally I would not have to look very deep to see his pain, I know, but now the pain is lying right on the surface . . . he just carries it along there with him, like you would carry a heavy jacket over your shoulder. His eyes are set close together under his brow, and they are wide open with the distance his mind is from the sidewalk. His eyes are brown, but not one brown. They are all the different browns that his skin is, textured, mottled, shadowed.

His nose, even thought it's a plain, average nose, is an angry nose. The nostrils are flared, and the creases moving down from the edges of the nose to the corners of the mouth and beyond are shiny wet with the sweat of his exertion. His mouth is a tight black cut in his face. The thin lips are compressed together, pushed against each other, and I can tell that the teeth behind those lips are clenched by the power of that square jaw. The silent scream on his face is ready to leap from those lips, and I wonder if he ever lets it escape.

I am watching a bent, twisted, crippled black man make his way toward me on that hard sidewalk as his eyes slowly come back into focus, rise up to meet mine, and see me for the first time.

He stops at the curb, straightens up as much as he can, and looks from me sitting in my police car, to the red light, then back to me. His eyes now radiate pure challenge. He jams his fluttering hands into his ragged pockets, watching to see if my eyes leave his or follow the hands. *What about my hands?* ask the eyes. *You see somethin' wrong with my hands, man?* I just look at him, my chin resting on my fingertips, my eyes open ... neutral. He drags one foot off the curb, and once it is firmly on the pavement he drags the other past it and lurches into the street toward me. He needs his hands out of his pockets to help him balance his twisted frame as he moves his legs, but he has jammed them into those pockets to keep them from fluttering in front of me and he won't pull them back out. With his elbows stuck out on both sides he stumbles just a bit, then takes another step, and then another. *I didn't stumble man, I didn't stumble*, scream the eyes, *I'm walkin' 'cross this damned street jus' like everybody else, man. I didn't stumble.*

Our eyes are locked together as he moves nearer the front of my car. I feel a thousand powerful emotions at once watching him but I keep my own eyes neutral and unchallenging. He sees me watching and he looks hard for my eyes to show my embarrassment for him, or my mockery, or my pity. His eyes dig into mine, looking for the laugh. *You laughin' at me, man? You laughin' at me 'cause I'm black and bent and spastic? Goddammit, don' you laugh at me, white man.*

As he gets to the front of my car his right hand jerks uncontrollably out of his pocket and flutters around like a rubbery spider for a few seconds before resting lightly on the hood of my car as he drags his reluctant legs through another painful step. My eyes don't go to the hand but stay on his own eyes as they widen slightly and scream *I din' lean on your car, man. I don' need to lean on your car or anybody's car. I can cross this street without leanin' on your honky fuckin' police car*, and he lurches forward, trying to hurry.

As he moves slowly past the front of my car I only need to move my eyes to follow him, but his eyes must be ripped off mine unless he chooses to turn his head. He can't turn his head because he would be physically acknowledging that I exist, so like burned skin being torn from a wound his eyes leave mine and turn straight ahead, toward the far curb. He doesn't lose sight of me though. The side of his head, his ear, his clenched jaw, the wet shiny skin stretched over the tight neck muscles ... his whole being still watches me, still challenges me, still asks, *So what you lookin' at, man? Don' be lookin' at me 'cause there ain't nothin' wrong with me. Don' look at me, man.*

As he goes by I see a dirty handkerchief and a section of folded-up newspaper sticking out of his right rear pocket. It's the classified section, folded again and again and I can almost see the ads: Help wanted, no exp. nec. Labr. needed, must have car. Janitor. Cement. Lawn man. Paint. Garbage. Maintnc. Good man needed. *That's right, man. I can work. I don' need nothin' from you, man. I don' want your white welfare. I can work.*

I watch as he gets halfway across the curb lane, fifteen feet from the sidewalk on the other side. The red light changes to green. Engines rev up tentatively and he is right in front of a big old shiny Buick with three young black guys sitting in the front seat. The driver of the Buick, a skinny guy with a large afro, says something to the other two and they all begin to laugh. The crippled black man in front of them hears the laughter but his head doesn't turn. I can see he's really trying to hurry now and he almost falls, maintaining his precarious balance only by yanking his other hand out of the pocket and swinging both arms in sweeping arcs, the hands fluttering wildly. The three young guys in the Buick start howling and yelling at this and the driver gives the horn a long blast. The bent feet finally make it to the curb and I can see the back of his sweatshirt is wet as he rotates his hips awkwardly to get up onto the sidewalk.

The Buick slowly moves past him, the guys in the car still yelling and laughing. I still watch his back, knowing now I will see that seething head turn, knowing now I will see those laser eyes flash toward the Buick and tear through the metal skin of the car and incinerate its occupants. The anger, pain, and humiliation I know is there will now be condensed into a weapon, and he will lash out at his tormentors and destroy them, and when he has reduced them to charred meat with his eyes I will call a city truck and have the mess washed into the gutter.

But no.

The head doesn't turn. The eyes don't flash. I watch the stiff back as the shoulders slump and the head hangs down. The muscles in his neck are twisted and knotted but I see his head hanging down and I know his eyes are back on the sidewalk. His arms hang limply by his sides and he lets his hands flutter away unrestricted.

We have fired into him with our white phosphorus bullets with telling effect.

Cars move around mine as I sit there and watch him move away from me and I think, what about that hole in your pants leg, man? What about those want-ads? Where were you when your eyes stared so intently at nothing? Can you go back to that place? Is it a place you can run and laugh and be free? Will you find a job? Will you have a friend? A woman? Can you ever get an even break, man?

Hey, man... I didn't laugh at you. I was just looking, that's all.

As he shuffles through the trash beside the dumpster next to the chicken place I begin to drive away. I don't know if he knows I'm still there, still watching him, but as I watch he jams both hands deep into his pockets again, hunches his back, lifts his head, and looks straight ahead.

What are you lookin' at, man? You see somethin' funny? There ain't nothin' wrong with me... so what are you lookin' at?

Forty-Nine

THE SERGEANT, preparing to go on duty with the south end midnight shift, pulled on his tight-fitting shiny black leather motorcycle boots. The boots had heavy metal cleats on the heels that made a clicking sound as he walked down the hallway to briefing. He walked with his back very straight and his shoulders squared. He had been a marine officer in Vietnam, he had been a cop for many years, he had recently been promoted to sergeant and had qualified for motorcycles, and now he was going out on that big Harley-Davidson to supervise his men on the shift.

The neighborhood drunk climbed awkwardly into his old Chevrolet and fumbled with the keys. His T-shirt was dirty and the zipper was open on his faded work pants. He had had a few beers after work and then had gone home to hear his wife start on him about money. No money, no air conditioner, no cigarettes, no new shoes, no nothin'. He was a bum, had always been a bum, and couldn't even make it in the service. Hell, everybody knew he had been kicked out of there and had never been able to do anything since but drink. He had cursed his wife and driven to one of the neighborhood bars where he knocked down more beers and the occasional shot, even though he couldn't afford it. He had said something wrong to some broad sitting on the next stool and the next thing he knew the bartender had him by the belt and the back of his shirt and had hustled him out into the parking lot. So now he was in his Chevy, and if he could get the damn thing started, get the keys in the ignition, he would drive to another bar off State Road 84 he knew about. At least the people were friendly there.

The sergeant rode easily on the big Harley, enjoying the power of the bike, the solid ride, and the feel of the night breeze against his face. He kept his back very straight and looked proud. He *was* proud. His helmet, his leather gear, and those beautiful boots all shined brightly in the streetlights as he cruised unhurriedly through town. It was getting late so the traffic had thinned. Not much on the radio either. It was just a good night to be a cop-sergeant-hog-Harley driver out on the streets fighting crime-and-or-evil.

The neighborhood drunk couldn't figure out what was wrong. He knew the car was running but the damn thing wouldn't move. He revved the engine again and heard some noise and felt the car rock slightly, but he still didn't drive out of the lot like he wanted to. He looked over his shoulder, peered through the back window, and saw a large garbage dumpster tilted right up against his rear bumper. Now what the hell? Then he bent down and looked closely at the gearshift indicator on the steering column. *R?* Shit, the stupid car was in reverse. He pulled it into *D*, revved the engine again, and found himself rolling smoothly toward the highway. He bumped over the sidewalk, crossed two lanes, and finally got the Chevy straightened out and headed east on State Road 84.

The sergeant turned off Federal Highway, westbound on State Road 84, when the alert tone sounded on the radio. He bent closer to the radio speaker clipped to his shirt and heard the dispatcher advise of an alarm at one of the businesses further west along the highway. He heard her assign two zone units to the alarm and then ask if there were any other units that could respond. The sergeant reached up with one hand, pressed the transmitter button, and told the dispatcher that he would head that way. He would set it up. He would respond.

There was an alarm, and the sergeant would respond.

He had responded so many times in the past. He had been needed, and he had responded. And now he was needed again.

The neighborhood drunk gripped the wheel and looked with

watery eyes through the dirty windshield of his car. He was eastbound in the center lane of the highway, and as he crossed the FEC railroad tracks he saw that the light was green at the next intersection. Andrews Avenue. Yeah, and he could turn there and head toward the middle of town and slide into that old bar he knew where everybody was easygoing and there was no bullshit. Then he thought about another bar on South Federal Highway, hesitated, and remained in the center lane, eastbound.

The sergeant gripped the handlebars tightly, twisted the throttle, and felt the power surge through the big bike, causing it to pick up speed rapidly. This was an alarm he was going to, not a parade. Some citizen was trying to make a living by running a small business, and he had spent money to install an alarm in case some maggot predator tried to break in and steal from him, and now that alarm was going off and the sergeant was responding. The sergeant increased his speed as he rode the Harley westbound toward Andrews Avenue. The light was green, and the only other traffic was a car eastbound, but over in the center lane. The sergeant looked through the intersection and mentally prepared to take the big bike across the railroad tracks just beyond.

The neighborhood drunk decided to go to the bar up on Andrews. The light was still green and he knew he could make it if he hurried. He stepped on the gas and whipped the wheel left, sliding out of the center lane, through the left lane, across the turn lane, and into the intersection itself.

The sergeant had time only to stomp and grab the brakes, and then the Harley-Davidson came together with the front of the Chevrolet. The Harley and the Chevy and the drunk came to an explosive stop right there in the middle of the intersection. The sergeant left the Harley, and the force of the impact carried him seventy feet before hurling him headfirst into a huge concrete lightpole.

He was dead before his body crumpled to the sidewalk ten feet below.

Fifty

"WHY ARE you calling me here at my home? I mean, I don't mind talking to you, but this might not be..."

"I called you because what happened down on Hollywood Beach, or what *didn't* happen, is making me crazy. I need to talk."

"We'll talk, this just isn't..."

"You're attracted to me, I know it, and I'm for *sure* attracted to you... and we go down there and things got so nice so fast and then you just *stopped*. Why? What happened? You would hardly even talk to me before you said goodnight and went home."

"Believe me... I wanted you, but..."

"But what? You're a cop with a wife at home who doesn't even know who you are. At least I know *who* you are, at least I *care* about who you are..."

"I know, and I feel it, all right? I think about you twenty-four hours a day too... but I'm *married*. I'm a married cop, remember?"

"Do you think she's being straight with you while you're trying to act like Sir Galahad? You've told me about all of her college friends and teachers and stuff. Do you think she's saving herself because she's still married to you?"

"Look. It doesn't make any difference. My feelings are all in a jumble right now, and you'll never know how difficult it was for me to stop it the other night. I don't know what is happening or where we're going, all I can say is I'm *married*, and..."

"Look. Let me know when you get it sorted out. In the meantime you'd better take a close look at who's being played for a fool."

Click.

"Who was that, honey?"

"Just a friend from work. Nothing important."

"Hey... why so glum?"

"Nothing, really."

"You know what I think? I think you need to go on another one of those crazy fishing trips for a few days with your buddies from work. Blow it out, have some fun, get away from the homefront for a while."

"Yeah. maybe. I don't know."

"Anyway, I'm off. A group from school is going up to Horton Galleries in Palm Beach today. Should be fun." Pause. "I'll probably be home late... some of us are getting together at Professor Wright's place for pizza and learned conversation."

"No problem, I'm working an extra detail tonight... late."

"Oh."

"Professor Wright is the young, tall, good-looking one, isn't he? The one you find so easy to relate to, the one you find so interesting and knowledgeable? He has these little gatherings at his place often, doesn't he?"

"Whoa. What's with the accusatory tone here? It's just a school thing, really."

"School thing. You've been spending so much energy doing school things you don't have any left for doing husband-and-wife things..."

"Oh, don't start that again. Has it been that long? Is it in my marriage contract somewhere that I'm supposed to please my husband so many times per week? Whether I'm ready or not?"

"Maybe I'm not learned enough, or interesting anymore."

"Maybe you're *not.*"

Silence.

"Um, look, honey... I've got to go now to get to Palm Beach in time. I won't be *real* late, I promise. Then maybe we can talk about it."

"Yeah."

"And listen, I just want to say, just want you to know, that with the way things are going, so little time for us to be together and all . . . the way it's been between us lately . . . well, maybe if there *was* a chance that you could share a few minutes of . . . gratifying time . . . with someone else, I'd understand. What I'm trying to say is I'd understand if . . . something happened, if you felt you needed . . ."

"Oh? And have *you* shared a few minutes of *gratifying* time with someone else? And you want *me* to understand because *you'd* understand? Because you felt you needed . . . ?"

Long hard looks, bitten lips, eyes turned away. Then back.

"You don't understand anything I talk about anymore. You look at everything with your cop's eyes, wrapped up in your cop world." Pause. "I don't think I want to be part of that world anymore . . ."

"What? C'mon . . ."

"No. I'm going now, I have to go . . . we'll talk later. But don't you see what's happened? And what's going to happen soon? It's inevitable."

Fifty-One

THE INFLUENTIAL citizen's son damaged a tire on his car while fleeing at high speed from the sergeant who was trying to stop him after he was observed driving recklessly. The influential citizen's son had already had his driver's license revoked for other violations, but here he was again, out tearing up the streets in his big car. He had some buddies with him and may have been showing off. Whatever. When the sergeant attempted to pull him over he led the sergeant in a high-speed chase all over the south end. He finally managed to lose the sergeant with a wild turn across the median strip on State Road 84, but in doing so he damaged a tire. A few seconds and a few blocks later I picked him up and continued the pursuit down Andrews Avenue. The chase went for a few more blocks and then the big car swerved out of control, sparks and blue smoke flying, and skidded to a stop at the edge of the road.

Even though the Fort Lauderdale PD tried to provide its officers with the latest equipment for the job, none of the patrol cars at that time were equipped with magic crystal balls. None of us knew why the influential citizen's son had fled from the police so violently and recklessly. We didn't even know he *was* the influential citizen's son. Why had he led us on this crazy dangerous chase all over the place? What crime had he and his buddies just committed? Was it a stolen car? Was the trunk full of drugs, or a body? Had they just pulled an armed robbery, were they armed and dangerous, were there felony warrants out on them?

It was all going on in my mind as I slid my patrol car to a stop behind the influential citizen's son's car and jumped out. I drew my revolver, crouched, and yelled for them all to freeze. Both doors popped open and the driver started to get out. The front seat passenger didn't move, but the two guys in the backseat crouched down as if hiding. Why?

The driver continued to get out and stand up. I yelled at him to freeze but he stood to his full height and leaned against the open door of the car. The driver was the influential citizen's son. As I approached him with my gun out and advised him again to freeze, he moved toward me. The other guys in the car began moving around. The influential citizen's son got closer. He was very big and heavy, six-four and over two hundred pounds. He smelled of alcohol and his eyes had a wild look as he reached out for me with his long arms and big hands. I stepped back, but he kept moving toward me with his arms spread wide.

Based on what I had seen to this point there was no question of using deadly force. The guy was definitely big enough to hurt me if he got hold of me, but I saw no weapon, and so far I had no knowledge of a felony. I holstered my weapon and prepared to physically control the influential citizen's son. I wanted him spread in the pat-down position against the rear of the car; that way I could control him and still keep an eye on the interior of the vehicle while I waited for my backups, who would be there in seconds.

The influential citizen's son came closer with his arms wide and lunged toward me as if to grab me in a bear hug. I tried to take his right elbow and turn him toward the car but he would have none of it. He used all of his strength to turn against me and then lunged again, towering over me and coming down toward me strongly.

I did not hit the influential citizen's son. I did not kick him. I did not pistol-whip him (as I was later accused of doing by his lawyer . . . this was totally ridiculous. I loved my service revolver too much to chance damaging it on some asshole's head). I *did* channel all of the influential citizen's son's strength, which he would gladly have destroyed me with, in another direction. He came to me, passed by me, and literally *dove* with great élan and enthusiasm, face first into the asphalt pavement of the street. His nose was the first thing to make contact, and it was followed with great force by the rest of his large body. His nose had served him well for years but it just wasn't up to this task. It was crushed, broken, destroyed.

Turned out the car wasn't stolen, and no one else in the car had done anything wrong. The influential citizen's son had been driving on a revoked license and had fled from the sergeant to avoid further trouble. Everyone was sent home, the influential citizen's son was taken to the hospital for immediate repairs, and eventually booked, and that was that.

That was that until the ten thousand dollars in plastic surgery was completed on the nose of the influential citizen's son. That was that until the influential citizen sued the city for his son and won a ten-thousand-dollar settlement. That was that after the influential citizen's son plead guilty to all the traffic charges and was acquitted of the resisting arrest charges I had placed on him. That was that until the situation was used to add to my reputation as an officer who used his hands or his feet or his gun too fast.

Maybe I should have let him grab me and tear my shirt, or hit me in the face, or pull me down under him to the asphalt. Maybe I should have let him hurt me before I stood him on his nose.

Oh well.

Fifty-Two

SHE LAY on her back on the harsh black pavement of the street. Someone had made a pillow of her light blue sweater. She was conscious and gazed with clear eyes up into the bright sunshine. Her gray hair had been elaborately coiffed and shined slightly silver-blue. It did not appear mussed at all, and her makeup, which enhanced her eyes and rosied her cheeks, was all in place. In her right hand by her side she held a small white clutch purse, and around her neck was a pretty string of pearls. Her dress was shiny blue with a small collar and no sleeves. She had a thin white belt around her middle and the hem of the dress came to just below her knees. She wore flesh-colored stockings that made her legs look thin, and she had no runs in them even though both legs were dramatically broken just above the ankles. While she lay flat on her back her feet were pointed sideways, at right angles to where they should have been. The stockings, designed to stretch, had compensated for the strain of the impact and now flexed nicely at the horrible bend in her legs.

Her sky-blue shoes lay a few feet from her in the street.

I knelt beside her and gently laid my hand on her forehead as the EMTs roared up and jumped out of their unit. She felt my touch and her eyes found mine and she smiled warmly at me as if to say, There there... everything will be fine. As she looked at me she reached up with one hand, took mine in hers, and gave it a squeeze. As the med guys gathered around her I stood and backed away slowly, looking the hundred feet down the road where her husband lay.

He was not on his back, or his side either, but in that curious twisted way completely destroyed bodies do. He had been covered with a yellow emergency blanket but it had been blown off his head and I could see his wispy white hair waving slightly in the breeze. His right arm was outstretched and the pink hand was balled into a fist.

I stopped backing when I bumped into the van that had impacted the couple as they attempted to cross North Ocean Boulevard. It sat in the middle lane, facing south, frozen in the street where its tires had run out of skid marks. The impact damage was in the exact center of the front of the van, from about shoulder height down to the bumper, which was dished in nicely right where their lower legs had touched it. The driver of the van was sitting on the curb, holding his head in his hands.

I looked at her when she spoke. She asked about her husband, Is he all right? Several voices at once all said, Yes of course he's fine don't worry he's okay. As I listened I looked to where the old man lay twisted on the pavement and watched as the A.I. slowly went around the body spraying yellow paint from a can, making an outline of the final resting place on the street. Incredible, horrible artwork... his own personal painting, a lasting, poignant statement from him to the world.

She spoke again and I looked at her small feet in the stockings and thought of how she had gotten herself all dressed up to go out dancing with her husband. When she let him escort her out onto the floor she wanted to look nice. I remembered watching the old ones at one of the big hotels on the beach where there was a dance band and a ballroom setting. The men were stiff and proud and correct and the ladies positively radiant. As they danced together you could see the years of trial and happiness they had shared, the failures and the victories and the private moments. They moved their bodies together publically when they danced, it was important to them, and they enjoyed it. Gravity and time had tried to drag the women down, but they had fought it and survived and they were dressed up and with their men out on the floor dancing for themselves . . . and for others to see them and admire their completeness.

There was a short discussion between the EMTs and the AI and he quickly and quietly took the paint can and sprayed an outline of her legs while the feet were still turned at that terrible angle. He only sprayed up to her hips and she didn't notice but I saw that some of the yellow paint fell like dust along the edges of her blue dress. As the AI moved away one of the med guys motioned to me and I knelt beside her with him while his partner slid his hands gently down her legs to her ankles. We held her shoulder firmly and watched her eyes as he moved one, then the other leg, slowly back into its correct position. She didn't move, and I could see she had no idea her legs were broken or that she had even been touched. The airbag splints were fitted into place and as they brought the stretcher beside her she suddenly tried to sit up and turned her head to look toward her husband. What about my husband? She asked and we all told her not to worry he was okay and he would follow her in another ambulance, and she lay her head back on the sweater and softly cried because she knew then. I watched her cry silently for a few seconds and then slowly backed away, got into my unit, and drove off, not looking at her or her husband as I passed them by.

With all of the commotion at the scene her little sky-blue shoes were left lying in the street with the bandages when everyone cleared. Someone had come along and kicked all of it over against the curb and there they lay day after day as I drove by on some call or another. Late one afternoon on a quiet shift I stopped there and walked to the curb and stood looking down at the bandages and sky-blue shoes. I looked out into the center lane and studied her play-doll yellow outline painting, looked into the clear sky for a moment, and saw the old couples whirling and turning on the dance floor. I looked at the shoes again, and kicked them down into the rain gutter, where they fell with two small splashes.

Then I got back into my unit and went away.

Fifty-Three

I WORKED an undercover narcotics assignment for a while, and was attached on temporary duty to a countywide task force run by a Broward County Sheriff's Officer major who would someday be the sheriff. The major was a cop, and he genuinely enjoyed pursuing bad guys, especially upper-level drug smugglers. At that time it was considered bad form by our own State Department to suggest that the Bahamian government was involved in massive shipments of drugs into the US...that members of the Bahamian cabinet, all the way to the top, knew of routes and shipping and airstrips and protection for the smugglers, in exchange for tons of cash. The major knew it to be true and reasoned that if criminal conspiracies were being hatched out of our country, and these conspiracies would eventually result in the breaking of our laws *here*, then we local cops could go out of our jurisdiction to work the cases. It was sincere, it took guts, and it made us headlines...if not favorite sons of our own federal operatives throughout the Caribbean.

I was promoted to sergeant just before being sent to the task force, and almost all of my police experience was street-related. I was never comfortable being "undercover," and I admire those cops who can slip into the second skin like it was their own and stay and work in that slippery and dangerous environment, case after case.

Undercover work: I spent the day with an informant on Andros Island, trying to get a local supplier to front me cocaine that the Bahamian customs officials had taken from other smugglers and were now selling on the open market. I was the only cop there, the deal fell through in bad humor, and when I got to my small airplane and told the pilot to get us out of there an official jeep driven by an official captain parked in front of our turning propellers, blocking us from taking off. I waved for the captain to come around to the cabin door, and when he moved the jeep I told the pilot to go for it. We were pretty sure shots were fired at us as we sped down the small runway. When we re-entered the US and prepared to land at Pompano Beach, a swarm of US Customs officers descended on us, weapons drawn. A Bahamian had dropped a dime on us after we flew away from Andros.

I sat around a hotel pool on Bimini late one night with a couple of heavy smugglers as they discussed my group providing transportation for one hundred kilos a week into Florida. It was a new organization, but I was made to feel better when the top guy smiled at me and said, "Don't worry about infiltration . . . I can smell a cop a mile away." On another trip with this same group I lounged on the flybridge of a sportfisherman halfway across an impossibly blue Gulf Stream on a perfect sunny day, enjoying the sight of the several beautiful girls the bad guys employed as window dressing lounging around the boat naked. The top bad guy wheezed his way up to the flybridge, sat next to me, and told me he'd pay me five thousand dollars if I'd kill his partner there and then. His partner was below, smoking and joking, and had somehow angered the top bad guy. I could kill him right there and dump him over the transom into the depths and that would be the end of the crud, said the bad guy. I became indignant, offended at having been offered so little for the job. The bad guy just shrugged but retained my partners and me long enough for us to make a case on him anyway... and his partner did eventually wind up extremely dead.

One big nasty enforcer for a group told me to my face once that if I turned out to be a cop and tried to arrest him he would kill me. He was big, bad, and always carried a Browning high-power automatic... and he would kill me. After I spent the night in suspended animation with eight hundred thousand dollars in cash for forty-three kilos of cocaine in the trunk of my car, we took the bad guys down. The enforcer backed against the trunk of his car, went for his gun, and I shoved the barrel of mine right up his left nostril. As he contemplated this one of my partners blindsided him, took him down, and we all did the Bristol Stomp on his head. I've got a great eight-by-ten glossy of this enforcer standing there after we picked him up, the front of his trousers stained with his own urine. I figure my partners saved his life by taking him down when they did.

I also spent some time assigned to the Harbor Patrol Unit, piloting marked and unmarked police boats through the many waterways of the "Venice of America." We used the police boats to fight smugglers too, working with Customs, blockading Port Everglades, chasing racing boats in our skateboards or tying up alongside large luxury yachts so stuffed to the gunwales with dope they actually wallowed in the waves. I drove around in my police boat in the early morning or evening, admiring the sun. I bantered with fishermen and assisted tourists in rental boats. I waved at pretty girls and admired their forms... and the whole time I felt restless.

I became more disillusioned as I worked the bigger narcotics cases. I saw the double and triple standard within our system, and I saw the perversive effects huge amounts of illegal and liquid money can have on that system. I stood there with a tiny tin spoon and tried to shovel shit against the tide, and felt the futility.

I longed for the street.

Fifty-Four

DUTCH WAS the kind of undercover narcotics cop that movies are made of. He was young and healthy and good-looking and muscular and intelligent and quiet and tough. He was street-smart, educated, and experienced. He believed in the job he was doing and gave it one hundred and ten percent at all times. At home he was a loving and caring father, with a beautiful wife and daughter. His wife worried about him, but never inhibited him in the pursuit of his mission.

On the street he was legend.

When Dutch began his undercover career, police agencies were just gearing up, blindly, for the upcoming war on narcotics in the South Florida area. He walked into the vice squad and the sergeant gave him twenty dollars and told him to go out and "buy some dope." He used his own car, wore his own clothes, and sometimes used his own money. Soon other agencies wanted their new guys to work with him because of what he was learning out there and how effective he was becoming. In a world where police officers were still excited about finding a baggie of grass or breaking up some one-hundred-dollar deal, Dutch was intercepting pounds of cocaine, bags of Quaaludes, and tons of marijuana.

The Fort Lauderdale police recognized what they had in Dutch. They encouraged him, sent him to school in Washington, promoted him, and took credit for his many exploits.

Dutch had a total dedication to what he saw as his mission. Long before we saw overtime pay he put in brutal hours on hard cases. His wife had been a hairdresser, so Dutch's appearance would change drastically all the time. One night he'd have long straight blond hair and mirrored sunglasses. The next, curly black hair, a bandana, and granny glasses. His chameleonlike antics fooled many a dealer, even the most paranoid. He even busted the same dealer twice in two days, driving the same car! He believed in what he did, and the public that paid their nickel to have a narc on the street definitely got their nickel's worth out of Dutch.

Dutch was promoted to sergeant and given the narc squad as his to run. His men respected him and worked hard for him, and they became an effective team. That type of unit is always changing players, cops come and go (again, here Dutch was legend for having been undercover longer than any cop known). When new people came into the squad Dutch would try to teach them and help them along. He couldn't always *pick* who was assigned, though.

Dutch got a new guy, a cop with a short time in patrol, relatively raw. Often this was good because a new guy didn't yet have that cop look. With help and encouragement and time the new guy managed to put together a small deal, and the squad prepared to work it as a team. The new guy had gone through an informant to meet two guys who would sell him some cocaine. It was a small amount, and there were the usual delays, but finally the night came for the meeting. The new guy would hand over the money in exchange for the coke and then the backups would swoop in and arrest everybody. Simple enough.

Dutch's squad was busy with other deals but he pulled in enough men to work the new guy's buy. Dutch briefed everyone to make sure they knew their positions and jobs. Then he sent them off to get whatever equipment they would carry. At that time officers on special jobs could carry almost any weapon of choice as long as they had qualified with it on the range. The narc squad was becoming more progressive, but at that time still kept a throwback from the old days: the gun closet. In this closet was a pile of guns from the small .25 autos to big revolvers and sawed-off shotguns. Some of them had been there for years; in fact, it would take in-depth investigations later to find who had placed the weapons there, where they had come from, and who had cut them down if that was the case. On that night the men went to the closet, grabbed what they wanted, and went out in teams to converge on the area of the buy-bust.

That night Dutch's partner will be a guy I'll call Cain. While Dutch assisted the new guy with the bodywire, Cain loaded his equipment into Dutch's car. Dutch and Cain would take up a position a block away from the buy to observe the action with binoculars and listen in on the bodywire receiver. They would give the move-in signal. This was the new guy's first time up front, and Dutch wanted it to be as much of a controlled situation as possible.

Dutch drove his car and Cain sat with his equipment on the passenger side. Cain had been a cop for about seven years at that time. He was very tough and ballsy and excitable and physical and violent. He had a temper and was quick with his hands. He had a reputation for questionable handling of firearms, and had already been reviewed by the Shooting Board. He was explosive and volatile (before I am judged too harshly for my description of Cain, let me admit the same things were said about me. I worked with Cain in the northwest long enough to know. We worked well together, he and I, we both liked to kick ass when we could. He had a temper and he was tough, and so did I and so was I, and if he reads this he'll know it's true). Dutch and Cain eased into position in the dark, made visual contact with the scene, picked up the voice of the new guy on the wire, and waited.

It was a ripoff all the way. The dopers never had the cocaine, but they counted on the long-hair to have the money. They planned to take it from him, and were ready to kill if necessary. The meet took place in a parking lot next to a low-rent apartment building. The two dopers came out and stood with the new guy. There was the usual discussion: "You got the shit, man?" "Yeah, you got the money?" "I got the money, but I gotta see the shit." "That's cool . . . I got the shit, but I gotta see the money, dig?" and so on. Finally one of the dopers turned to "go get the shit." During the conversation the other doper had managed to ease around to the side of the new guy, and when his partner turned he hit the new guy in the head . . . with a brick.

The new guy went down.

Dutch and Cain had observed this and they headed that way as Dutch gave the move-in order. They slid into the parking lot and Cain jumped out the right side and ran to the new guy who was sitting up, yelling, "They're running!"

During the short scuffle the new guy lost his .25 automatic. It was gone, he didn't know where, so he advised the others he thought one of the dopers was armed with his gun.

It was night in the alleys behind the yards, over the fences, in the bushes, and they searched for two guys who had just hit a cop with a brick and were armed with his gun.

Adrenaline time. Fear time. Anger time. Physical time.

The new guy caught one doper, and Cain was right behind him. The doper struggled with the new guy and then was dumped onto the grass. Punches were thrown, vicious words grunted. The doper was handcuffed, and the new guy ran off in search of the other one. Cain stood over the handcuffed doper laying on his belly in the grass.

Cain held a sawed-off over-and-under twelve-gauge shotgun. The gun was over twelve years old, and the barrels had been cut down years ago. Cain stood over the doper with his chest heaving from exertion and anger. His jaw was clenched and he gripped the weapon in his hands tightly. The doper struggled on the ground, and Cain screamed at him to lay there or die . . . something like, "I'll blow your fucking head off!"

Dutch came around to the rear yard where Cain and the suspect were from a different route. He needed information. He knew one suspect was in custody, but his men were still searching in the dark for the other one. He ran around a corner of the small apartment building to where Cain stood over the doper. He asked Cain what the situation was.

Cain turned his body, holding the shotgun across his hips, to respond. The doper on the ground struggled. The shotgun went off.

The entire load of twelve-gauge buckshot travelled three feet, cut across Dutch's right thigh, gouged out a large chunk of muscle and nerve tissue from there, and then impacted Dutch's left inner thigh just below his groin. The blast of the powerful weapon lifted Dutch and hurled him backwards onto the grass. The roar was deafening. He lay on his back looking into the night sky, wondering what had happened.

The next segment of time for Dutch was one of hell, of pain, of terrifying fear. Screaming... Cain was kicking the fence and screaming. Fire... his legs were on fire. Blood, he would bleed to death. Voices, orders shouted, screaming confusion. In the chaos Dutch lay on his back in the grass, brought his radio to his lips, and advised the dispatcher he had been shot and needed an ambulance. He gave calm orders, he brought the situation under control.

Cain screamed.

Dutch's wife got the knock on the door in the middle of the night, and she knew. Two guys from Dutch's squad were there, and she knew. She rode to the hospital with them.

At the hospital Dutch told anyone who would listen that he didn't want them to take off the leg, no matter what. He was reassured, but the nurses and doctors and brass looked at each other and shook their heads. The left leg was smashed, destroyed, the femur bone broken in at least five places, with immense nerve and muscle damage. They knew the leg would have to come off. Dutch, still conscious, told them again and again... the leg must not come off. They smiled and shook their heads, but they all knew better.

All but one.

A visiting doctor heard about the cop-shooting. He went to see. He had been a combat surgeon in Vietnam, and was fa-

miliar with traumatic wounds. He offered to make an attempt
to save the leg. Dutch's wife was told they *might* save the leg,
but Dutch would probably never walk again, or in the very least
he'd be a cripple.

Eight months to the day after he was shot, Dutch walked back
into his office on light-duty status. He walked with a cane, and
he favored his left leg. But he was there.

Dutch's story should make a book, and probably will. It would
take a book to tell how he struggled against the pain and the
inevitable addiction to painkillers while he lay in a full plaster
body-cast for months. To tell of how his wife had to care for
him, alone, twenty-four hours a day. To tell how he fought being
a cripple by dragging himself from his bed the day after the
cast was cut off, how he forced his body to move, how he created
his own physical therapy at a private health club he had to pay
for himself. It would take a book to tell of how his family suffered
mentally and emotionally, of how they fought, and of how they
are still fighting.

It would take a book to tell how the city deserted him.

He was like me and a lot of other guys on the job. We knew
the dangers and accepted them. We knew we could get hurt,
and sometimes did... but we also knew our city, our police
department, would look after us and our families if that happened. We knew that the city administration and the police
chief would make sure we received all the medical attention
and follow-up therapy we would need. We knew the brass would
come around checking on us, helping us, making sure our
paychecks kept coming in so we could feed our families. We
knew we had been working our guts out all those years, doing
crazy things, taking chances, hurting ourselves emotionally so
the city would be safe. It sounds corny, but we knew in our
hearts we fought for the right things, that the people needed
us... and we knew we would be cared for if we went down.

We were wrong.

*　*　*

Dutch had to fight every inch of the way for every single thing that should have been his automatically from the beginning. He finally—and reluctantly—had to get an attorney and fight the city in court just to get the basic benefits needed to keep his family going. He had a choice of lying there, waiting for help from his supervisors, or fighting them. He fought... and the fight took its toll on him and his family.

A short time after Dutch walked into his office with his cane he was told he was being transferred. He was the most experienced narc sergeant in the area, the most respected, and he wanted to work, to get back on the street. His job as narc boss had been promised to him by the chief, who had a reputation as an honorable man. His job would still be there, he had been told. He came back, through the expenditure of more guts than that same chief ever had, and found himself transferred to the inside, an administrative job. Cain was promoted, and Dutch was told he was a cripple, a liability, and an embarrassment.

Dutch resigned from the department shortly after that, and will never work as a cop again. He tried to keep believing in it all, but it just couldn't be. When Dutch left the job for the last time the citizens of Fort Lauderdale lost a good man.

We all lost one.

I had worked with Dutch when he and I were both young and fairly new patrol officers. We were casual friends through the years, respecting each other, hearing of the other's exploits, occasionally bumping into each other in the hallways or out on the street on some operation.

I became true friends with him after he was shot. I visited him in the hospital, and later at his home... just to show support, to be one of his fellow officers who made a show of caring about him and his fight to regain his health. During those visits, which after the early weeks became a lonely vigil, I was witness to his abandonment by his supervisors and the city.

My casual time with him, and my friendly display of support, was turned into a crusade by what I saw happening to him and his small family. When it became obvious that *someone* had to make a phone call, when *someone* had to speak out, when *someone* had to actually cajole the funds and then go rent a walker for Dutch's rehabilitation, I did it. I didn't want to be a crusader, and I didn't want to go to war with a city administration I had butted heads with in the past. But as the weeks went by and I sat at Dutch's bedside, more and more often alone, seeing him fight, seeing his anger and frustration and disillusionment, seeing the simple and frightening injustices being done to him, I had to act.

I stood beside him emotionally and physically as he fought his fight, and what I saw and heard through those years scarred me more deeply than I knew then, and peeled away the last shreds of naivete from my eyes, searing them with the harsh reality of betrayed loyalty, fraternal disappointment, and professional abandonment.

The truths I learned during Dutch's fight for his dignity and pride helped me make a wrenching personal decision a few years later. Even in accidental wars between brothers, there are casualties.

Fifty-Five

"OH, OFFICER, he wasn't like those other boys at all. Not this one. I mean, he was so sweet, so...quiet. Oh, I know what you're thinking, but really, he was different. I didn't even meet him like I've met some of the others, at least not right off the *street.*"

I sighed, looked around the tastefully decorated living room,

and asked, "Where did you meet him? And I'll need a description."

"Yes. Well, the way I met him was simply *marvelous*. Oh,
can I get you something, officer? A cold drink, coffee? Something *stronger?* No? Well, please don't hesitate to ask, okay? I
mean, you *have* been here before for this sort of dreadful business haven't you? Anyway, I was practically *forced* to attend
what I just knew would be a totally *boring* dinner party given
by a couple I know over on the beach. You know the type, very
avant garde and simply *wild* with their money, but no class
really, no *feeling* for taste, if you follow me."

I looked at the beautiful polished teak coffee table and the
one perfectly balanced bowl of orchids that sat on it and shook
my head.

"Well, let me get *on* with it. I do find you so easy to talk to,
officer, that's why I asked for you by name when this terrible
situation developed. Honestly, I've been positively *distraught*
trying to deal with this myself, and people can be so *cold* sometimes. So... yes, the party. Well. I was standing there listening
to one of my friends positively *gloat* over this new boyfriend
they'd acquired, a big, sunburned muscular thing, really. You
know the type, probably an absolute *Trojan* in bed, but after
that dull, dull, dull. In order to escape from my friend's intol-
erable *strutting*, and quite frankly feeling a little lonely and
sorry for myself, I carried this old masterpiece into the kitchen
for more wine and a respite. And there he was. Simply lovely,
not real big and tall, maybe just above average, and not beefy
either. Athletic, but in that *sleek* way, know what I mean?
Carried himself so lightly and smelled so fresh and clean and
had such a soft, interesting voice. Oh my."

"Hey... easy now, crying won't help." I said softly, "Here,
take a sip of your water and calm down. Now is the time for
you to be strong so we can get the info we need to find your
car and the credit cards."

"Yes. Yes, you're right, of course, officer. I must be strong.
Thank you. Ah, there, that's better. Oh, officer, it's just that
when you get to be *my* age and lovers have come and gone and

you look back through all the years at all the times you just *knew* this was the one. Oh, it's so difficult. All those lovers, and there I am *still* alone. And, well, let's face it, officer, at my age we tend to *fall apart* a little, you know, *sag* a little here and there, and it becomes so *hard* to make new friends. And then you *do* so want to trust people..."

I looked at the perfect nails and the styled hair and the beautiful cream-colored sweater and said, "Oh, I think you look better now than the last time I saw you. You shouldn't get down on yourself because of this, you're still a very attractive person."

"Oh, Oh, officer, how very *nice* of you to say so. *My*, you'll get me flustered and we'll just *never* get through this. You know, he had brown eyes like yours, very soft but bright at the same time. Well, there we were in the kitchen together and he poured my wine for me and our hands touched and I looked at him and would have brought him home and let him use me in *any* wild way at that *instant.* He was just *too much.* We talked, the time flew, I told him all about me, and the next thing you know we were leaving together! It was so fast, and so *wonderful.* He just left his date standing in the driveway, calling after us ... well, you *know* that caused a bit of a stir in *my* circle! I loved it, of course."

"Shame on you."

"Oh, I know, officer. You're right, shame on me, but it was so *exciting.* And that night, and almost *all* of the next day, and then *that* night. *Well.* Marvelous, just marvelous. I don't mean to be risqué, officer, really, it's just that I want you to understand how *special* this was. Well, by late last night that boy had just used me *up.* Totally. I was just *spent.* But happily, I must admit. And I slept, slept like an old parlor cat, stretching and purring and *everything.* And then of course this morning I wake up and the only thing left of him is the scent lingering on the sheets. Ah, yes. Of course he *would* take my car, I love it so. The credit cards I can deal with, heavens knows I've dealt with it before. But my lovely little car. You have the paper there with all the little numbers on it, and I told you the color and everything. He mentioned Miami to me several times, officer, he said he had friends there. Maybe that's where it will turn up. Oh dear, I hope this one doesn't end up like the last one, simply *stripped*, remember? I was crestfallen for *days* that time."

"Yes. Well, let me get to work on this," I said as I stood and stretched. "My report will list the credit cards also, and the description of the car will go nationwide. It would serve this one right if you decided to press charges this time when we find the car, but I won't ask you to make that decision now. Listen, I'm only a cop, and I can't tell you how to run your life, but I think you should try to exercise more caution when you meet new friends. Go slower, check them out first, get to know them before you bring them home. Know what I mean? No one likes to be alone, or lonely, but if you're not careful you'll just keep getting hurt, and that's no good either."

He reached out, touched me lightly on the arm, and said quietly with a little smile, "Yes, you're right, of course, officer. I'm just a lonely old fool. But he was *so* lovely."

Fifty-Six

SHE WAS right. What happened to us was inevitable. I had become a man focused on a world she could not know and no longer tried to share, a world where even my victories concerned the conflict of negatives. She had become a woman thirstily drinking in a world she perceived to be without limits, a positive place full of promise. We had both cheated, maybe physically, certainly emotionally and intellectually. We turned our backs on each other's world in equal parts of fear, selfishness, hope, and a desire for identity, potential, and reason.

We had no child support payments, alimony, or large property settlement to argue about, so our divorce was quick, friendly, and brutal. Our small home went up for sale, proceeds to be split, and we both moved out and went in separate directions. Even the dividing of the household things was carried out with exaggerated courtesy and concern.

I moved to a small apartment on the east side of town, near the water. I acquired a cat, two beanbag chairs, and a bedspread emblazoned with lions and tigers and bears. I covered the naked windows with tin foil. My landlady was pleasant and caring and pleased to have a cop for a tenant. Within a week I traded in my old beat-up VW for a brand-new Firebird with tinted windows and a big mill under the hood. I bought some new clothes, a can opener, and a clock radio. I opened a new checking account in my name.

She was gone, I was a divorced cop, and I drove around town in my macho Firebird feeling a hard cold aloneness creep into me. I felt tickled by a curious freedom, but wasn't sure if I would fly or just withdraw into myself, peeking out only to examine with cynical skepticism anyone peering in on me.

Fifty-Seven

NOT ALL cops ride a police motorcycle during their careers. It is a voluntary assignment, traditionally prestigious, and usually an officer must submit a letter requesting the assignment and then wait until there is an opening. The motorcycles are part of the Traffic Division, and the primary function of the motor-men (or motor officers) is traffic enforcement, traffic control, and accident investigation. They are expected to write tickets, and because they are very mobile and focus on traffic problems, they can usually write more tickets in a day than road patrol cops. Rarely are there quotas. We used to like to answer any question or accusation about quotas with, "Quotas? No... we can write as many as we like..."

This is not to say that motormen stop being police officers. They have the range of the whole city, instead of being assigned one zone. They listen to their radios too, and if a felony call comes out, or an officer in trouble, or something that just sounds like a goody, then they can kick it into gear and roar off toward the scene. Motor officers are often in the thick of things because of their mobility in heavy traffic... they can *get* there.

I have always been fascinated in the change that seems to come over a "regular" cop who gets a motor assignment. The change even happened to me during the time *I* rode those big chargers, and I reveled in it even as I recognized what I had become. The change can be seen in the officer's self-perception and attitude. To be astride the bike, out there in traffic, wearing a gun and a badge, is a wondrous thing, a compelling moment in a cop's life, a time of vanity and confidence.

I loved it, did it for almost a year, and then left it to climb back into a battered patrol car smelling of fear and vomit, to immerse myself again in street police work. But there was something superfine about riding a police motorcycle. We had that big old Harley-Davidson hog then, and it was solid and heavy and tough and beautiful. Being a motorman wasn't just a job, it was a state of mind. You were special, and it was important to always look and act like it.

When you rode motors you were spit-shined, you were perfect. Your creases had creases. Your helmet shined, your boots were like glass, your pants were spray-painted on, your leather, including the Sam Browne belt, gleamed, and your mirrored sunglasses rebuffed any inquisitive glances inside. Your body was tough, sun-bronzed, and hard, you walked with a boot-stomping swagger, and you rode your bike with your back straight and your powerful fists locked on those handlebars.

That hog Harley was a beautiful monster, and its engine made the most incredible solid mellow rhythmic sounds you ever heard. God, it was something . . . not like those big sewing machines the guys are riding now. It's just not the same.

Anyway, how about the time John and I are riding together up in the north end, cruising, looking tight, looking good. We get a call to handle a fender-bender on Oakland Park Boulevard, near the phone company building. We ride that way, gleaming in the sun and exuding macho confidence.

We arrive and pull into the parking lot. Our helmeted heads turn toward the building in unison to see that some kind of shift change is taking place. The front of the building and the sidewalk are busy with a whole gaggle of young women. They are pretty and colorful and looking at us and hell, we are motormen.

In formation we pull the big bikes, engines pounding nicely, into a parking space side-by-side. In formation we shut them down and swing off the seat. In formation we turn and begin to walk with perfect macho supersharp measured tread toward the crowd of helpless adoring females.

Ah, yes.

We get a few gleaming steps away from the bikes when we hear a horrible loud crashing sound. We stop. We turn slowly. We see that John has forgotten to put his kickstand down, and his hog just stood there on its fat tires long enough for us to walk away before it fell over on its lovely side.

Shit.

Without looking over our immaculately tailored shoulders we walk back to the scene of the mechanical faux pas. We are trying hard to look nonchalant, as if we knew it was going to happen and in fact had *intended* for it to happen. Now we would show how easy it was for two lean motormen to pick up a usually proud representative of the Milwaukee iron works. Sure.

We did get it back up on its kickstand, and I guess we made it look easy. Strength through embarrassment. Neither of us got a hernia, so we turned to walk back to where the fender-bender was waiting. Incredibly, all the young women had gone off about their business.

Oh well.

Or how about the time John and I came off the beach and were westbound on Sunrise Boulevard, looking good as usual. We came up on Bayview Drive and decided to ease into George English Park to sit in the shade for a few minutes. We turned right onto Bayview, still in perfect formation, looking *so* good, and idled our gleaming way to the entrance turn-off. I hung back to let John make his left turn into the park. There was moderate traffic so John slowed slightly, and then hung it, laying it over beautifully and bringing it out and up straight without even so much as a wrinkle in his perfect shirt. It was enough to bring tears to your eyes.

My turn. I waited until there was a break in traffic and swung it hard over. You don't just make a left turn when you are a motormen. You lay that hog over and curve all that power into the direction you are headed. You sort of *become* the turn, if you know what I mean, the very *essence* of the turn is you and that Harley. Phew.

Well, I laid it over so far the kickstand bracket on the bottom of the frame contacted one of those reflector diamonds in the pavement. Oops. Down I went just as easy as you please. The bike skidded off to one side and I wound up sitting on my butt in the street.

It is very difficult to be gleaming macho superfine when you are sitting on your ass in the road.

John stopped and looked and I jumped up and waved that I was okay. Then I ran over, grunted that hog back onto its tires, jumped on it, and rode it out of the street. As I did I heard horns blaring and people yelling and saw some people staring at my macho motorman's behind. When my practically perfect rear end made contact with that evil pavement my skin-tight motorman's pants could not take the strain. They blew out . . .

they just *shredded*, leaving me with my ass hanging out for the world to see.

Sometimes being cool is a very difficult thing to do.

From George English Park over to Luigi's tailoring shop is only a couple of blocks, but it was one of the longest and breeziest rides I ever made.

Fifty-Eight

I WAS working day shift, northwest, mostly the black section of Fort Lauderdale. Normally we rode two men to a unit in that area in those days, but for some reason I didn't have a partner that day. I was assigned a mostly residential, usually quiet zone. I was supposed to take it easy, handle any reports that came along, and get through the shift.

It was a quiet day, and I was bored. I drove around one of the side streets and there, coming the other way, was a black kid on a small motorcycle. The kid was fourteen or fifteen, had no helmet, should have been in school, and was riding what just had to be a stolen motorcycle. Trust me.

So I stopped in the road and as he approached I waved for him to pull over. He slowed, but kept coming. When he was close I began to climb out of my unit to speak with him. He grinned at me and took off down the street with me yelling after him to stop. I jumped back into my car, turned around, and went after him.

There are chases and there are chases, and I guess you could call this one hot pursuit. There he was going hell-for-leather down the street on his motorcycle, and there I was roaring along behind him with my lights flashing and siren screaming. We went through the neighborhood like that, around and across and over the streets. There was no traffic, and no pedestrians. I was sitting back, driving one-handed, feeling slightly silly about the whole thing. The motorcycle wasn't fast enough to outrun my patrol car, but as long as the kid kept going, all I could do was follow along. Reluctantly I advised the dispatcher I was in pursuit, and heard her start the search for backup units.

I saw the kid look over his shoulder and begin to slow down. Then he hung a left, went off the street and into the yards between two houses, trying to cut across to the street on the other side. It would have been all right but the yards were just soft dirt and trash. He made it halfway, with my Plymouth right on his ass, and then the bike went down under him. I was coming through the sand, and if my momentum was maintained I could have made it through to the street beyond. But when I saw him go down in front of me all I could picture was that monster Plymouth crashing down on top of that stupid motorcycle and that stupid kid. Shit. He would be crushed under the car and killed for sure.

I slammed on the brakes.

The Plymouth dug in and stopped inches from the motorcycle, and as it did the kid jumped up and began running off across the street, into another yard, and behind another house. I jumped out of my unit, looked at the bike lying there, and took off after him. I chased that kid for about ten blocks through the yards and over fences and into hedges and around houses. By the time I lost him I was a gasping, disheveled, scratched, and torn wreck. He was last observed westbound at a high rate of speed, not even looking over his shoulder to see if the honky po-leeseman could keep up. He couldn't.

I didn't feel too bad as I trudged along the sidewalk, making my way back to my car and the motorcycle. I had lost my suspect, but at least I had his ride, and if it was stolen then I had recovered it. If it wasn't, then I had deprived the kid of its use until somebody came in to claim it with an explanation.

With those thoughts in mind I made my way across the dirt yard to the Plymouth, only to see that the car was still hunkered down comfortably into the dirt, and the motorcycle was gone. I stood with my hands on my hips and looked all around me. Quiet. No one in sight.

And the motorcycle was gone.

I guess I could chalk up the whole thing to experience. I cleared the radio and prepared to get on into the station and clean up before end of shift. I sat behind the wheel of the Plymouth, started it up, put it in drive, and felt it bury itself to the rims in the soft dirt. Then I asked the dispatcher to send a wrecker to drag the unit out of the yard and back to the pavement.

I sat behind the wheel and examined the situation.

A short while ago I was the white knight, the main man in his charging steed of steel. What had been a powerful bronze police unit carrying the white knight from one mission of truth to another was now a giant planter, and what had once been the white knight was now a cross between a sweaty Raggedy Andy doll and an asthmatic marathon runner with an empty snipe bag.

I rested my head on the steering wheel and said softly, "Rats."

Fifty-Nine

"WELL, LOOK who's here, mooning into his Irish whiskey...
the recently divorced and thus liberated macho cop and super
cockhound!"

"Hey, guy... how's it goin'?"

"Me? The same, always the same, man. First wife's bitching
for money for the kids, second wife's bitchin' about *havin'* kids,
and my friggin' girlfriend is wringing me out from both ends.
But why complain? Things are normal."

"Yeah..."

"Shit, man, you look glum for a guy that's reputed to be
screwing every pink thing that'll hold still for it! I've heard
you've left a wet trail through half the bedrooms in this city...
makin' up for lost time with a vengeance. I even heard there
was a new demand for chastity belts, fuckin' firefighters are
afraid to go off to work, knowin' you're out there, cocked and
loaded!"

"C'mon, man..."

"What happened to that sweet thing from Records who was
trying to polish your knob before you got divorced? Everybody
thought you two would be an item, you know?"

A long sip of whiskey.

"Uh, we're just trying to be friends now. It was good, it really
was. I mean, I was like a thirsty man at an oasis with her. Then,
just about the time I get my apartment set up the way I want
it, she comes on big-time about movin' in with me... wanted
to live together, wanted to see if we could look at a future."

"Uh-oh..."

"Uh-oh is right, man. It bummed me out. Hell, I don't even know who I *am* right now. I sure as shit don't want to start talkin' about the future."

"I hear ya, man."

"So here I am with my face stuck in this Bushmill's, trying to mind my own business."

"Time to go reclusive, huh?"

"In a way, man. I mean, I want to taste them *all*, you know ... there's plenty of hydraulics, friction, and lubrication to be experienced..."

"...Amen."

"...but beyond that, no way. I'm *in* here somewhere, and nobody's gonna look in there for me until *I* look in there and see me..."

"Damn, man, sounds complicated to me. In the meantime take a look down the bar there at the two that just came slidin' in here. Fine, fine, fine."

"My, my... and the one's already lookin' at me with those ride me if you can' eyes. I do believe I can already taste it..."

"Yeah, man, welcome back to the world."

Sixty

"HEY, MY man . . . just stand right there a moment. We need to talk."

"Why? What's wrong, officer? I didn't do nothin'."

"Yeah. Let's see some I.D. How about a driver's license since I just saw you pull up in that sweet ride of yours. Break out the registration too."

"No problem, officer. Like I said, I'm clean. Here you are."

"Okay, let's see . . . you be Mr. Tyrone James, and this be your seventy-eight Cadillac Bro-ham, right? Very good, Mr. James. Now tell me, what do you know about these whores that are walking up and down north Federal Highway here?"

"Why, officer, I don't know nothin' about them whores. That ain't my business, no sir, don't know nothin' about it at all."

"That right, Mr. James? Well, let me tell you somethin', okay? You is a motherfuckin', scum-suckin', shit-eatin' *liar*. I've been doing too much checking around, Mr. James, uh-huh, that's right, talkin' to the girls after they been busted, and watchin' *you*, my man. The word is, you is the *pimp*."

"Wow, man, be cool, okay? I don' know where you're comin' from. I done tol' you I don't know nothin' about those whores."

"Yeah. You just walk back this way, away from the door of your car, and make yourself comfortable. I've got some guys from my squad comin' over. I want them to get a look at your sorry ass. See, Mr. James, after our little meeting here you're gonna be *gone*. I ain't gonna see you *or* your little whores on my streets again, know what I mean?"

"I don't know what you're talkin' about, officer."

"Hey, sarge, what's goin' on? We all came as soon as we could."

"Good. Who's got that Polaroid? Okay, listen. This here is Mr. Tyrone James, and this is his sweet ride. I want you all to get his tag number and write down his D.O.B. and any other info you want from his DL. My man here is the pimp that's been working these ladies on the sidewalks in the evenings."

"Oh yeah, remember last week that one chick told us about Tyrone?"

"Yeah, and the vice squad guys had a thing on him too."

"I heard about him from one of the motel managers down the street."

"You'd think a pimp that was makin' all that money on his girls wouldn't have to dress like a fag, know what I mean? And man...does he smell."

"All right, Mr. James, just stand up straight and smile for the camera, there ya go. And another one...and wait, there, one more. Good."

"Look, officer, I don't know..."

"Right, asshole. You don't know, but you're gonna learn right now."

"But officer, that's my driver's license...don't do that."

"There you are, Mr. James. Now whereever your car goes, your DL will go along."

"But officer...you put my license in the gas tank."

"That's right, asshole. And now listen up...and you guys listen up too..."

"Let's hear the word, sarge."

"The word is that by tonight there will be no more whores working this area of town. I have good info that says if you stop Mr. James here driving his Caddy he will *not* have his DL on him. If he drives with no license you'll have to arrest him and tow away his car. Also, pass these photos around to *all* the guys. I want to be fair about this so make sure every cop working out here knows this dickhead. Here's the deal. We know how dark it gets out here in these parking lots and alleys at night. Lord

knows sometimes it's hard to tell if some scroatbag you're checking out has a gun in his hand, or a knife. If any of you guys
come across Mr. James here, and in the performance of your
duties you are forced to blow his ass away, I will personally see
that you get a couple of days paid vacation."

"Now wait a minute offi—"

"Hey! Great, sarge, real good—"

"Yeah, I hope it's me!"

"Hey, sarge. What if we just can't set it up to blow him away?
What if we can only manage to beat the piss out of him, and
burn his bro-ham to the wheel hubs?"

"Oh. Well, in that case I'd buy your dinner that night."

"Okay, that's fair."

"Good. Look, you guys can split now if you want. Pass the
word on our Mr. James here, and keep an eye out for him."

"Sure thing. See ya, sarge."

"Now then, Mr. James, we're almost finished."

"Look, officer, really, I mean . . . you're just jivin' me, right?
Playin' with my head a little? You can't do this. You can't stick
my driver's license down the tank of my car, you can't say these
things to me, and you can't tell your men to kill me or beat me
if they get a chance."

"Guess again, Mr. James. The vice squad guys are out here
all the time on citizen complaints, trying to have your girls
proposition them so they can make a legal bust. Then of course
there's no room in jail for that kind of shit, so the girls are right
back out in the morning. Hell, every once in a while they'll
even get female officers out here to bust the johns that try to
pick them up, hoping the arrest and the guy's name in the
paper will be a deterrent. Lots of manhours are spent trying to
get your girls off the street. Go ahead, asshole, tell me it's the
oldest profession in the world, tell me it's needed, and I'll tell
you about the robberies and knifings and drugs and clap and
filth that goes with it."

"But officer . . . you can't . . ."

"I *can* and I *will*, motherfucker. I'll do whatever I must to
make you go away. When you leave, the girls leave, it's that

simple. I don't give a *shit* about the methods, get me? Yes, the ends *do* justify my means. *You*, shitbird, have the word. Get your girls off the streets, and get your sorry ass and your shiny Caddy and your cheap clothes out of my sight, or they'll find you in a dumpster man, a *dumpster*."

"Officer, you're... crazy..."

"Correct, Mr. Tyrone James. I am very crazy, and I will do what I have to do. *Whatever* it takes. Goodnight."

Sixty-One

ACONOMIE HAD the gun.

He held it warm against his skin under his shirt as he and the two men with him climbed out of their big white Cadillac parked along the side of the convenience store in the southwest section of town. As the three of them walked away from the car a young white guy backed a pickup truck next to them and parked. In the back of the truck was a load of fresh corn. The three of them looked at it lying there and the young guy told them to help themselves if they wanted some. Then he turned and walked into the store. Aconomie and his partners waited a few seconds, looked around, then went into the store behind him.

It was the end of a quiet evening shift for me, almost eleven o'clock, and I was on my way into the station. The night in the north end of town had been peaceful, and as the sergeant of the squad up there I had very little to do but listen in on the Tactical channel as the Tactical Felony Squad followed a carload of robbery suspects around the city. The suspects appeared to be casing convenience stores for a hit, and every time they would sniff around one the Tac boss would have the dispatcher tell all the marked units in that area to stay clear until after the robbery went down. They didn't want to spook them too soon. It had been going on for hours, many stores had been cased, and now they were looking hard at one in the southwest. They had parked their Caddy and were going inside, and the Tac guys had taken up positions at various points around the intersection where the store was located.

It sounded like it was going to go down, the Tac guys were tense and ready, and I was listening in as much as I could while monitoring my own channel. None of my people would be involved, and even though I couldn't be there it was still exciting to listen to the play-by-play as it developed. My stomach was tight and my palms sweated . . . and I was just listening.

Aconomie pulled the gun, pointed it at the girl behind the counter, and told her he would blow her head off if she moved. Then he pointed it at the young guy and told him the same thing. One of his partners made the guy lie on the floor, and took three dollars off him when he was down. Aconomie told the girl to get down also, and she did, and then the money was grabbed from the register. It was less than sixty dollars. They were ready to go then and Aconomie was charged with the excitement and power he held. As his two partners ran out the door he pointed the gun at the girl laying on the floor and fired. He missed, the bullet crashed into the floor and bounced away. Then he turned and followed his partners toward the Caddy.

"It's going down!" came over the radio as I pulled my patrol unit behind the station next to the fuel pumps. Then, *"Shots fired! Officer down . . . officer shot!* Suspects are fleeing in their vehicle north on Thirty-first Avenue! *Officer shot!"* I swung around the pumps, sped through the back parking lot, swerved out onto Broward Boulevard, and headed west.

When Aconomie and his two partners ran out of the store and toward their car the Tac guys began to move in, but most of them had been forced to take up positions too far away. They had left their cars, and were on foot. The closest one was Don.

He was in an alley between the rear of the store and the side of a music shop. He was near the Cadillac as the three suspects jumped into it. The car's engine was starting as Don ran out from the alley with his shotgun and began yelling at Aconomie and the other two to stop. Aconomie was sitting in the right front seat and saw Don coming. He stuck the .38 caliber pistol in his hand out the window and began firing. The first slug hit Don in the upper right leg and spun him around. As he fell another bullet hit him in the rear hip. Don went down hard onto the pavement of the parking lot and the Cadillac roared north on Thirty-first Avenue. Some of the TAC guys ran up on foot, firing with no results at the fleeing car. Then they ran to see how badly Don had been hit.

Anytime there is a chase or a shooting or an in-progress felony the radio becomes filled with tense voices, and the stress level is high. With this one a cop had been shot, and the culprits were getting away. Things were crazy. As I crested the top of the I–95 overpass and looked west I could see another patrol car, its lights flashing, pull onto Broward a couple of blocks ahead of me. It was a patrolman named Paul who had been working a traffic accident when the shooting went down. He had left it, and now he was hoping like me to somehow find the guy who had shot the cop.

The police airplane was in the air and had been helping Tac squad with the surveillance of the three suspects. The officers in the plane now advised that the white Caddy was still north on Thirty-first, and as they said it I looked west, and off in the distance I saw the blur as the Caddy crashed through the intersection with Broward, still going north. I followed behind Paul as he threw his car into a skidding turn north on Twenty-seventh Avenue. We would not have the suspects in sight, but would parallel their path. As I followed Paul I knew he was thinking the same thing I was . . . if the suspects continued their path they would drive into the heart of West Fort Lauderdale's black section. Once there if they bailed out of the Caddy we would have a good chance of losing them. And they had shot a cop.

Paul and I were still racing north, one squad car behind the other, and had just crossed Sistrunk Boulevard when the guys in the plane advised that the caddy had turned east on Sunrise Boulevard. We approached Sunrise with our sirens howling and our lights flashing against the parked cars and startled faces alongside the road. We got to the intersection of Twenty-seventh Avenue and Sunrise Boulevard in time to see the big white Caddy roaring in from our left. It entered the intersection in a brake-burning, tire-squealing turn, and headed north right in front of us. As the car careened through the turn the right rear door flew open for a few seconds, and I believe the guy in the rear seat was going to attempt to jump out while he had a chance. He didn't, and he would have died there if he had.

At this point in the chase a great sense of calm came over me. I had experienced it before during other violent, dangerous situations. I was racing through the night at seventy miles per hour in my patrol car, the siren and lights did their thing, and the radio screamed in my ear. But I was calm, and it was strangely peaceful. Paul was in his unit in front of me. He was a cop and I was a cop. We had worked together before and respected each other. I knew he could do what had to be done. Paul had been a marine in Vietnam, he wasn't a big guy, but he was tough. He was also a well-educated intellectual, and he would do what had to be done. He and I crashed through that night, drawn on by Aconomie and his partners. We knew a cop had been shot. We did not know if he was dead, or would die, or how bad he was hurt. We knew these three guys we chased were the shooters, the chase would end, and then someone would die.

The chase ended about seven blocks north of Sunrise Boulevard. The driver of the Caddy approached a *T* intersection in his roaring, speeding, heaving vehicle, and he hesitated. By the time he made up his mind whether to go left or right it was too late. All he could do was slam on his brakes and skid to a solid stop against a grass mound and a telephone pole. The Cadillac hunkered there in a cloud of dirt and dust and blue smoke.

Now. Now we'll see about shooting a cop.

Paul slid his car to a stop almost directly behind the Caddy. I swerved to the right and stopped thirty feet behind and to the right of it. As Paul opened his door he saw the guy in the back seat crouch on the seat and turn toward him. As I opened my door to move I saw one sweaty black arm flick out of the right front window, holding a gun. The gun fired back toward us once, and then the arm was drawn quickly back inside the car.

Paul, using his door for cover, began firing at the guy in the back seat. He hit the trunk of the Caddy (he was shooting with his left or offhand, because of his position) and then the rear window, and one of the slugs crashed through the glass and hit the guy in the face, just under the right eye. He went down.

While this was happening Aconomie made a fatal mistake. He had reached out and fired his .38 at the cops behind him, and then he crouched down on the seat behind the door of the car. He knew the cops would hide behind their car doors and yell for him to give up. He knew they would take up defensive positions and begin shouting orders at him. He crouched there on that seat with his head below the edge of the open window, and then he raised up quickly to see where the cops were.

When Aconomie raised his head he found himself looking into the eyes and gun of a cop who was running straight at him, screaming and firing.

A cop had been shot a cop had been shot a cop had been shot.

These bastards had shot a cop and we had chased them and now they had shot at *us . . . and now I was going to kill them.*

Instead of taking cover behind my door I moved. I had seen the guy in the back seat go down, shot by Paul. I couldn't see the driver but knew he was probably hunched down behind the wheel. I had seen the one in the right front shoot at me. I wanted him. I swung around my car door and lunged headlong at the right side of the Cadillac. I charged forward, leaning toward my target. I knew he would come up, knew he would have to look.

I had killed in Vietnam the same way.

When Aconomie stuck his sweaty face over the edge of the

window to look wide-eyed at me I was less than three feet away. My service revolver was tight in my hands, pointed at him. I screamed at him as I fired twice point-blank into his face. One slug hit the top of the window edge and broke up a little before spinning into his skull like shrapnel. The other slug took him dead on, between the eyes. His body was punched backwards and he was gone, out of sight.

By this time other units were sliding into the area and other officers were running up. I knelt by the side of the car and looked back to see Paul covering me. On the other side of the Caddy the driver began to get out with his hands up. One of the K–9 guys approached him slowly, gun drawn. The K–9 cop had left his dog in the unit, but as he tried to put the driver into the position against the Caddy the guy began struggling with him. Unbidden, the dog managed to squeeze out of the unit and came running to help his handler. The dog almost knocked the K–9 cop down getting to the driver. The driver was severely eaten . . . maybe the dog knew a cop had been shot too.

Then there was the usual craziness and shouting and orders and confusion and procedure and control and bright lights and blue lights and ambulances and captains. The area was roped off, and the usual crowd of people stood sullenly watching. The driver of the Cadillac was put in one unit, and the two right-side doors of the getaway car were carefully opened at gunpoint to see what was inside. The guy on the back seat was unconscious, with a bloody face. Paul and I dragged him out, laid him in the dirt, patted him down, and handcuffed him. Then we reached in for Aconomie. He was barely conscious, and the .38 lay on the floor of the car near his right hand. His face and head were covered with a thick oozing layer of bright red blood, and more was pumping. We pulled him out and cuffed him too. Then the EMS guys began working on them before they were transported to the hospital. One of the medics checked them both quickly, looked at Paul and me, and shook his head. "No way," he said. We just stared at him.

I flashed on that scene as we reached in and pulled the fluid bodies from the seats of the car, the way the bodies had that rubbery look, limbs loose as they slid into the dirt. It became juxtaposed with the bodies of North Vietnamese soldiers, long-sleeved dark green shirts, small backpacks, rubber sandals, and all.

When the scene was under control, the suspects taken away to area hospitals, brass and crime scene and detectives and sheriff's office detectives beginning their exhaustive criminal and administrative investigation, Paul and I eased off to the side and stood together quietly. The news came over the radio that Don was in the hospital. He had been hit twice, but he would be all right... the wounds probably would not cripple him.

Paul and I looked at the bullet-pocked Cadillac, at the thick dark blood on the seats and in the dirt, and into each other's eyes. Then we hugged each other, pounded each other on the back, stepped back, and said, "Yeah."

Paul was awarded Officer of the Month for his actions. Don recovered completely and went right back to work with the Tac squad. The driver of the Cadillac was sentenced to some good hard years in Raiford so all his dog-bite wounds could heal. The guy that Paul shot lived. The bullet had been slowed by punching through the rear window, and it impacted his face with enough force to knock him down and out, but not enough to enter the skull cavity to do real damage. He too received a long jail sentence. None of these guys were first offenders, they were hardcases with impressive records of felony arrests and con-victions.

Aconomie lived in intensive care with a brain full of lead for three days. Then he died.

The Fort Lauderdale police, the Broward sheriff's office, and the grand jury all found the shootings and homicide on our part to be justified. If Don hadn't been hurt in the process it would have been perfect. After he was back on his feet Don took me to lunch one day. We shared our views on those few seconds of police work that can make it all worth it, and he bought me a bottle of Bushmill's. He's still on the job.

I have relived that shooting in my mind many times since that night. I can still feel myself running toward the car, leaning forward with my service revolver, crashing down on Aconomie to kill him. He shot a cop and I killed him, and I'd stand in front of you or the face of God and say, "That's right, I did. *I did.*"

Sixty-Two

WORKING THE street for you and knowing the truth took their toll on me. I had the same problem many cops have; I believed in what I was doing. I would go out at night in my marked cruiser. I'd have a radio so I could hear you when you called for help. When it was *happening* you didn't call an attorney or a reporter or a judge or a city administrator or an influential person; you called me. I had a flashlight, the better to see you with, and I had a gun, because that's what the world has come to. I went out looking for that one who would steal from you, or hurt you.

You slept, and just outside your bedroom window were people who would violate your wife. They would steal your little girl and leave her body in a canal. They would smash their way into your business, where you have worked so hard to make a living, and take your tools. They would come into your house, your castle, your sanctum, and after they took what they wanted and smashed the rest they would defecate on your kitchen floor.

Who was out there to stop them? Me.

When you were afraid, I felt the fear. When you cried out I felt the pain. When you bled, I cried. I stood in your living room and felt your loss. The color TV set, your mother's ring, your daughter, she was only seventeen. When you were violated, I was violated. When you died on the hard pavement I knelt over you to keep the burning sun from your face. When I worked the street my uniform shirt caught the sun and warmed me through the cloth. I felt strong and right, and your powerful tin badge stood on my chest and gave me reason.

When you heard about what I did, or read about it, or saw it on the eleven o'clock news, it was already *history*. That minute capsule of time that existed only as I *acted* immediately began losing quality and purity and accuracy as the seconds and minutes and hours and days stumbled along behind it. Those respected and admired persons who later presented to you their version of the *act* were telling you of a history of something that happened in a land foreign to them, in a land of different languages, of different courage, of truth.

Often I was criticized or reprimanded for my actions. I kept on, however, because I learned that my critics were only hollow relics of what I represented. They fulfilled themselves vicariously through my courage, and the administrative and judicial combat they waged in the hallways, and the paper projectiles they hurled in response to my street results were but manifestations of their desire to control me. They had never known the street I knew, and they couldn't function there. Was I a rogue police officer, a renegade? Did I turn my back on our laws, ignore our system of rights and freedoms?

No.

I never abandoned the truth of the law. The spirit of the law remains pure, even as the letter of the law has been perverted by egotistical opportunists and sanctimonious and hypocritical overseers.

I took up your sword and hurled myself against those who would hurt you. When I was cut I bled like you. When I was killed, I died like you, alone. Every day my physical and emotional reserves were a little more depleted, every day another piece was torn from me.

Everything I did, I did for you . . . and I did only what I thought was right.

Sixty-Three

TO: Chief, Fort Lauderdale Police Department
FROM: Cherokee Paul McDonald, Sergeant
SUBJECT: Resignation

Sir:

I hearby submit my resignation from the Fort Lauderdale Police Department, effective immediately.

                              Sincerely,

                              Cherokee Paul McDonald